Making Markets and
Making Money

Making Markets and Making Money

◆

Strategy and Monetary Exchange

Bernard C. Beaudreau

iUniverse, Inc.

New York Lincoln Shanghai

Making Markets and Making Money
Strategy and Monetary Exchange

iUniverse, Inc.

For information address:
iUniverse, Inc.
2021 Pine Lake Road, Suite 100
Lincoln, NE 68512
www.iuniverse.com

ISBN: 0-595-32879-2 (pbk)
ISBN: 0-595-66700-7 (cloth)

Printed in the United States of America

To the memory of Jean-Charles Léonard Sismonde de Sismondi, Henry Ford and Edward A. Filene.

In the future a really big business success on the basis of mass production and mass distribution will be impossible except as it makes for both high wages and low prices… Low wages and high prices manifestly cut down that widespread and sustained buying power of the masses without which mass production sooner or later defeats itself. In other words, the business man of the future must produce prosperous customers as well as saleable goods. He cannot think of business as an adventure in getting money from the masses of people who, in one way or another for which he has no responsibility, have got money from someone else. His whole business policy must look forward to creating great buying power among the masses. Otherwise mass production cannot succeed. The business man of the future must fill the pockets of the workers and consumers before he can fill his pockets.

—Edward A. Filene, *The Way Out: A Forecast of Coming Changes in American Business and Industry*

Contents

Preface

This book examines the strategic aspects of market creation, where by market, it should be understood monetary income or, put differently, the ability to execute trades. Particular emphasis is placed on periods of paradigm technological change, where new general purpose technologies increase potential output without necessarily increasing costs. As income tracks costs, it stands to reason that actual income growth will be less than potential output growth, resulting in what I refer to as underincome. Potential output increases; however, the wherewithal to transform potential output into actual output, money income, does not.

Using game theory, it focuses on producer behavior in periods of paradigm technological change (e.g. steam engine, electric motor, information technology). It builds on two previous works, notably *Mass Production, the Stock Market Crash and the Great Depression: The Macroeconomics of Electrification*, published in 1996, where the concept of underincome was first introduced and used to explain the Great Depression, and *Energy and the Rise and Fall of Political Economy*, where it was used to examine the fallout from energy-based paradigm technological change in the 19th and 20th centuries. Specifically, it develops a formal model of producer-merchant exchange that is sequential in nature, and examines the properties of the resulting equilibria. The focus, put differently, is on what I refer to as the monetization of real (potential) output—specifically, on the process whereby real output yields (generates) its trade/exchange equivalent, namely money income. Despite more than a century of monetary theory, little is known of the strategic underpinnings of money and exchange.

I would like to thank, without however implicating, those who over the years have fostered my interest in this subject matter, notably Douglas Fisher, David Laidler, Don Patinkin, Robert Clower, and Peter Howitt.

1

Introduction

In recent times, however, the process by which new technological develop-
ments are transmitted into higher standards of living is obviously not work-
ing smoothly. Even before the coming of the great depression, there appeared
to be some doubt as to whether the system of wealth production and distri-
bution was operating with maximum effectiveness. At a time when cumu-
lative scientific knowledge might be expected to give us an accelerating
tempo of industrial growth, the rate of advancement for some reason, or
combination of reasons did not seem to be an increasing one. In any case, the
issue in recent years has been sharply raised: can the economic system be
counted upon to produce the beneficent economic results which were sup-
posed to be the automatic accompaniment of scientific knowledge, and the
increasing efficiency of production? Under modern conditions, do not tech-
nological improvements simply throw men out of work, destroy purchasing
power, and retard economic advancement?

　　　　　　　—Spurgeon Bell, *Productivity, Wages and National Income*

The development of the high-efficiency steam engine, by James Watt, in 1768, ushered in an era of universal optimism. The yoke of grueling, oftentimes physically-disabling labor had been lifted. Where man and muscle had toiled, now firepower would. As a result, the transformation of the earth's abundant supply of natural resources appeared to be unlimited. According to 19th century industrialist and social reformer Robert Owen, Great Britain's productive powers had been increased one hundred fold.

> It is well known that, during the last half century in particular, Great Britain.
> beyond any other nation, has progressively increased its powers of production,
> by a rapid advancement in scientific improvements and arrangements, intro-

1

duced, more or less, into all the departments of productive industry through-out the empire. The amount of this new productive power cannot, for want of proper data, be very accurately estimated; but your Reporter has ascertained from facts which none will dispute, that its increase has been enor-mous;—that, compared with the manual labour of the whole population of Great Britain and Ireland, it is, at least, as forty to one, and may be easily made as 100 to one; and that this increase may be extended to other countries; that it is already sufficient to saturate the world with wealth and that the power of creating wealth may be made to advance perpetually in an accelerat-ing ratio. (Owen 1817, 34)

David Ricardo shared Owen's enthusiasm, as evidenced by the following passage from *The Principles of Political Economy and Taxation*, extolling the virtues of machinery.

Value, then, essentially differs from riches, for value depends not on abun-dance, but on the difficulty or facility of production. The labour of a million of men in manufactures will always produce the same value, but will not always produce the same riches, By the invention of machinery, by improve-ments in skill, by a better division of labour, or by the discovery of new mar-kets, where more advantageous exchanges may be made, a million of men may produce double, or treble the amount of riches, of "necessities, conveniences and amusements," in one state of society that they could produce in another, but they will not, on that account, add anything to value. (Ricardo 1817, 182)

Roughly a century later, the development of the electro-magnetic motor revived early 19th century optimism. More flexible in its uses, and more amena-ble to energy-deepening (higher throughput rates) than steam power, electric power held out the promise of unlimited riches. According to Chicago power magnate, Martin J. Insull: "As a consequence of the added power which inven-tion has contributed to industry, the forty-five and one-half million workers in the United States have achieved an output equivalent to from six-hundred mil-lion to nine-hundred million workers before the power era." Matthew Sloan, president of the New York Edison Company, described the effects of electric power on productivity in the following terms:

Mr. Sloan compared this age which he termed the 'new industrial revolution' with 'the industrial revolution' of the eighteenth century, when the steamboat and the locomotive came into use. As steam brought in the machine era, elec-tricity, he said, has brought in the era of mass production which has so greatly affected the general economic situation and social conditions. Thus, electricity, he said, is responsible for our present production. With all its attendant circumstances of lowered unit costs, lowered prices, increased wages, intensified merchandising, wider markets, higher standard of living. Electricity-motivating machinery has multiplied the working power of the nation many times, he said, and the generating stations of the country now have a capacity of 35,000,000 horsepower, or the ability to do the work of about 35,000,000 men. In 1900, the generating capacity was only 3,000,000 horsepower. (*New York Times*, February 15,1929)

To some, like Stuart Chase, the problem was no longer scarcity, but, rather, abundance, specifically, the problem of achieving potential wealth.

Two men are lost on a great desert. One has a full bottle of water, the other a bottle quarter filled. As they move wearily onward, hoping for an oasis, justice demands that they pool the water supply and share it equally. Failure to do so will undoubtedly result in a fight. Now let us transport these two men to a row boat on Lake Superior. Again, they are lost, and again, one has a full bottle of water, and one a bottle quarter full. The full bottle man refuses to share and a battle ensues. Maniacs! There is plenty of fresh water over the side of the boat. The Desert is the Economy of Scarcity; the lake, the Economy of Abundance. The choice between sharing or fighting is chronic in the former, pointless in the latter. Today, throughout western civilization, men in boats are fighting, or preparing to fight, for fresh water. They do not know they are in boats; they think they are still on camels. The lake, as we have seen in the previous chapter, is not limitless, but nobody need go thirsty. (Chase 1934, 51)

Ironically, by the mid-1800s, the U.K. economy had experienced numerous downturns, some more severe than others, and, more importantly, the standard of living had fallen markedly. Wages, both nominal and real, had fallen by over 20 percent. By the mid-1900s, the U.S. economy had experienced the worst downturn in the history of material civilization, the Great Depression. In the early 1930s, one out of every three workers was unemployed. Real U.S. GNP had been halved.

This raises a number of interesting, and, until now, unanswered questions. For example, why did 18th-century and 19th century optimism turn to pessimism? After all, in both cases, a new source/form of power had been discovered/developed. Why did the U.K. and U.S. economies fail to make the transition to the new, higher growth path defined by their respective power revolutions? Why did real wages and real profits fail to increase?

In this book, an attempt is made to address these issues. Drawing on earlier work (Beaudreau 1996a,1998,1999a), I argue that the main cause was the presence of underincome, defined as the failure of nominal and real income to increase commensurately with overall productive capacity (potential output). This, I show, owes to the underlying structure of monetary exchange in an industrial economy. The latter is defined as an economy in which producers coordinate production and merchants coordinate trade activities in a multi-agent setting. In times of paradigm technological change (e.g. first and second industrial revolutions), there are no private incentives to increase wage income (nominal and real), which, given that profit income is a residual form of income (paid after product markets have cleared), resulting in underincome. Merchants, whose orders from producers are based on aggregate income levels, specifically, aggregate labor income levels, respond by not increasing orders for the incremental consumer and capital goods. The end result: poverty in the midst of plenty, and welfare reducing, employment-decreasing rationalization activity on the part of producers. Potential output exceeds actual output; potential income exceeds actual income. In time, the now more productive producers decrease employment, sending the economy into a recession, if not a depression. Thus, while in a barter economy, actual supply creates actual demand (Say's Law), it is by no means clear that in a multi-agent producer-merchant economy, potential output/capacity necessarily creates an equivalent level of money income.

This work differs from my earlier work in a number of important ways. First and foremost is the analytical framework used to study underincome. In earlier work, simple multiple agent/producer models were used. Here, drawing from recent work in the literature on uncertain and sequential trade (Bental and Eden 1996; Williamson 1996), I develop a formal model of producer-merchant exchange. This is then used to study the problem of exchange in pre-industrial and industrial settings. Second, the focus is on underincome, not on technological change per se, nor on the problem of distribution. My earlier work focused on the causes and effects of underincome, paying less attention to the underlying structural features.

The book is organized as follows. Chapter 2 presents the theory of underincome using a heterodox model of producer-merchant exchange. Specifically, I begin with a review of the literature on money and exchange, paying particular attention to exchange technologies. That is, the means by which goods and services are exchanged (e.g. barter, money, intermediated, and non intermediated trade). This provides the necessary segue into the model proper. The problem of underincome is then identified and analyzed in the context of technological change. Policy issues are then discussed. The results of this chapter constitute the analytical framework for Chapters 3 to 7 where underincome is studied in its many forms, including energy deepening-based underincome (Chapter 3), and non energy deepening-based underincome (Chapter 4). Non energy-based underincome refers to underincome that results from non energy-related technological change. An example of the latter is the current ICT (information and communications technology) revolution which, by reducing variable costs, has raised the spectre of underincome. With producers in the North reducing variable costs (labor), overall money income decreases, resulting in underincome. Heretofore, who will make the market? Chapter 5 examines the relationship between underincome and stock market prices, focusing on the U.S. stock market in the 20th century. As underincome is synonymous with untapped potential, it is argued that the observed gap between actual U.S. stock prices and their "rational" equivalents (Shiller 1981,1989) can be attributed to the presence of underincome. Chapter 6 examines the "competition versus cooperation" debate as it relates to what I refer to as the problem of "making the market." Chapter 7 broaches the question of the future, specifically the future of exchange in a world in which variable production costs, as a percentage of total costs, are asymptotically tending toward zero (i.e. owing to automation and globalization).

2

The Theory of Underincome

Despite the fact that bank notes or deposits are used in the daily business of hundreds of millions of people, there still remain numerous misconceptions concerning the nature of these media of exchange. Furthermore, it seems safe to assert that few indeed, not only the users but also of the bankers who issue the obligations, have any clear idea of just what effects upon the public such issues produce. According to the writer's observation, textbooks in economics rarely touch upon this last and most important phase of the problem. It therefore appears to be worth while to discuss in some detail the fundamental principles connected with bank credit. Bank credit is used mainly for business purposes. Some loans from banks are obtained in order to purchase consumption goods, but loans for this purpose form so small a fraction of the total that they scarcely need consideration here. The bulk of credit loaned, not only by banks, but by other lenders as well, is nowadays borrowed for purposes of investment or the use in the undertakings for profit making.

—Williford King, *Circulating Capital: Its Nature and Relation to Public Welfare*

2.1 Introduction

The problem of underincome, as defined here, is, first and foremost, an exchange-related problem, one that is inexorably linked to the nature of the game played by producers and merchants. Specifically, aggregate income, whether nominal or real, fails to increase commensurately with society's ability to produce, heretofore referred to as potential productive capacity, or simply productive capacity. Producers have no private incentives to increase wages, which, combined with the fact that profits are a residual form of income, paid out only when output has been delivered to merchants, results in income inertia, or simply, underincome.

This chapter outlines the theory of underincome. To this end, a parsimonious model of producer-merchant exchange is developed. Finding existing models of exchange (monetary, Walrasian) to be inadequate, I, following in the footsteps of 19th-century Swedish economist Knut Wicksell, develop a sequential producer-merchant model of exchange. I assume the existence of two sets of market coordinating agents, producers and merchants. The former coordinate production in factor markets, while the latter coordinate exchange in product markets. Both finance their transactions using costless bank trade credit.

2.2 Money and Exchange

It could be argued that money and its role in the exchange process is one of the oldest—indeed, the oldest—topic in economics, going as far back in time as the 16th century, when monks at the Universidad de Salamanca in Salamanca, Spain, studied the problem of species-induced inflation. Recent discoveries of gold in the New World ushered in decades of price inflation in the Iberian peninsula. This was followed by Jean Bodin's work on inflation in 17th-century France, and David Hume's work in the early 18th century. Add to this John Law's 1705 controversial work, *Money and Trade Considered With a Proposal for Supplying the Nation with Money* on the nature of money and wealth.

Unfortunately, interest in all things monetary waned for the most part in the late 18th and 19th centuries. Classical and neoclassical political economy was cast in real terms. Monetary issues were, for the most part, an after thought. Witness, for example, the classical dichotomy which divorced real from monetary issues (i.e. classical dichotomy). Money, it was argued, was, at best, a veil.

The resulting void and the breakdown of the gold standard in the early 20th century rekindled interest in monetary matters. Prompted by the breakdown of the gold standard in World War I, John Maynard Keynes, Gustav Cassel, and Irving Fisher began re-examining the role of money in the economy. The result was a series of theoretical developments that today constitute the core of monetary economics. These include the precautionary demand for money, the speculative demand for money, and price indexes, to name just a few. These early contributions were followed, in the post-World War II period, by numerous attempts at modelling a monetary economy, beginning with Don Patinkin's *Money, Interest and Prices* in 1958. In spite of these contributions, little was known of the so-called nuts and bolts of money and exchange. For example, most-if not all- of the models abstracted, for the most part, from production activity, the focus being on pure-exchange economies.

2.3 The Problem of Exchange

It is generally argued that the main economic problem is scarcity, defined as unlimited needs/desires in the face of limited resources. Microeconomics and macroeconomics examine the problem of resource allocation, itself founded on the problem of scarcity. Exchange, the process whereby goods and factor inputs are traded, is assumed to be frictionless, and hence, a non-issue (e.g. the Classical Dichotomy). For example, once output (value added, transformation, goods and services) is produced, it is assumed that its dual, money income, exists, and that, eventually, it will be spent (consumed or invested). Markets are assumed to exist, and, moreover, constitute a sufficient condition for exchange.

In this chapter, and, indeed, throughout this book, the opposite view is taken, namely that exchange and the exchange process have, are, and will undoubtedly continue to rank among the most important problems in western industrialized—and indeed, pre-industrialized—countries. Traditionally-defined resource allocation (production, distribution, and expenditure), consequently, is a second-order problem. The pitfalls of the first industrial revolution (recessions, depressions, a falling standard of living), I argue, were exchange related, specifically were the result of underincome. As pointed out earlier, underincome refers to the inability of private, Nash economies—of which the British economy in the early 19th century is the defining example—to generate income commensurately with productive capacity (Beaudreau 1999a). The Great Depression in the 1930s was the result of underincome (Beaudreau 1996a,1999a). I begin by examining exchange and the exchange process as currently modelled in economics.

2.3.1 Science and Exchange

How is exchange formalized in economics? How is it modelled? What is the relevant time framework? Who are the relevant agents? What are the relevant institutions? Surprisingly, microeconomics and macroeconomics, for the most part, ignore these questions. Implicit in introductory microeconomics and macroeconomics is the view that once value added (output) is produced, it is costlessly exchanged, and then consumed and/or invested.

This view is formalized in terms of the "circular flow" diagram of economic activity, where the exchange process is likened to a highway with goods and services going in one direction and money going in the other. There is no beginning and no end. Moreover, the highway is assumed to exist. There is no mention of its architects, its builders, and its maintainers. Goods and money spontaneously flow in opposite directions. In short, the classical dichotomy.

While useful as an overview of economic activity as a whole, it stops short of providing an empirically-consistent model of the origins of economic activity (i.e. Smith's notion of our innate propensity to "truck and barter"). Absent are the agents who make production and trade possible, namely producers, merchants, and bankers, the first coordinating production activity, the second coordinating trade activity, and the third providing the wherewithal for both, namely credit (trade credit)—what Williford King referred to as "bank credit." Producers coordinate production in a market setting, buying factor inputs, and selling the final product to merchants. The latter coordinate distribution, purchasing goods from producers, and selling them to the consuming public. This raises the question, why are merchants and bankers, as essential to trade as producers, virtually absent from mainstream political economy?

This is an interesting question, one which, unfortunately, extends well beyond the scope of this book. Suffice it to say that in the last century, a number of political economists have attempted to model exchange scientifically—that is, with an eye to the real world. One such economist was Knut Wicksell, who in *Interest and Prices*, published in 1898, presented a sequential model of exchange involving bankers, producers and merchants.

> We may assume further that production begins everywhere at the same moment of time, at the beginning of the economic year, which need not, of course, coincide with the calendar year; and we may assume that the final product, the consumption goods, are not completed or available for exchange until the end of the year. This would correspond in some ways to the situation of former times, when in many districts the exchange of commodities was concentrated on one, or a few, great annual markets.
>
> The total quantity of consumption goods is then the same thing as the quantity of liquid real capital in its free form; or rather it is the same thing as the quantity of this capital, inclusive of the amount with which the owners of capital have the right annually to credit themselves as remuneration for the capital employed in the previous year and which they consume on their own account during the current year.
>
> Our imaginary procedure is then as follows: At the beginning of the year the entrepreneurs borrow their capital from the banks, in the form of a sum of money K. This is equal to the value of the total amount of available real capital, that is to say, of the total amount of consumption goods completed during the previous years minus the interest drawn in the previous year by the capital-

ist. This money capital is now paid to the workers and to the landlords; and at the same time entrepreneurs allocate to themselves an amount as remuneration for their own labour, risk-taking, etc., and pay the normal competitive rents for such "rent-earning goods" (sites, buildings, machines) as may be in their possession. With the aid of this money, the whole of the available commodity capital is now bought up by the consumers and the, and the money capital K returns once again to the banks in the shape of the deposits made by the capitalist dealers. The goods are completed only at the end of the economic year, and it is only then that the entrepreneurs can meet their liabilities. It follows that the credit which is granted by the banks to the entrepreneurs partakes of the character of one-year loans. (Wicksell 1898, 139)

Others who attempted to provide empirically-consistent (i.e. more realistic) models of exchange in industrial economies include Clifford H. Douglas, the founder of the Social Credit movement. Consider the following passages taken from Douglas' *Monopoly of Credit.*

Let us imagine a capitalist to own a certain piece of land, on which is a house, and a building containing the necessary machinery for preparing, spinning, and weaving linen, and that the land is capable of growing in addition to the flax, all the food necessary to maintain a man. Let us further imagine that the capitalist in the first place allows a man to live free of all payment in the house and to have the use of all the foodstuffs that he grows on condition that he also grows, spins and weaves a certain amount of linen for the capitalist. Let us further imagine that after a time, this arrangement is altered by the payment to the man of £1 a week for the work on the linen business, but that this £1 is taken back each week as rent for the house and payment for the foodstuffs.

Let us now imagine that from the time the flax is picked to the time the linen is delivered to the capitalist, a period of six weeks elapses. Obviously, the cost of the linen must be £6, and this will be the price, plus profit, which the capitalist would place on it. Quite obviously only one-sixth of the purchasing power necessary to buy linen is now available, although "at some time or other," all £6 has been distributed.

Let us now imagine that half of the employee's time is devoted to making a machine which will do all the work of preparing and manufacturing linen, and that the manufacture of this machine takes twelve weeks. We may therefore say that the machine costs £6, the total value of the production of the machine and the flax being still £1 per week. At the end of the period, the machine is substituted for the man, the machine being driven, we suppose, by the burning of the food which was previously consumed by the man, and the machine being housed in the house previously occupied by the man, and being automatic. The capitalist would be justified in saying that the cost of operation of the machine is £1, per week as before, and if there is any wear, he will also be justified in allocating the cost of this wear to the cost of linen. It should be noticed, however that he will now not distribute any money at all, since it is obviously no use offering a £1 note a week to a machine. (Douglas 1951, 40)

In the modern industrial system, this process can be identified easily in the form of machine charges. For instance, a modern stamping plant may require to add 600 per cent to its labour charges to cover its machine charges. This sum not being in any true sense profit. In such a case, for every £1 expended in a given period in wages, £6 making £7 in all, would be carried forward into prices. Although this is an extreme case, the constant, and in one sense desirable, tendency is for direct charges to increase as a result of the replacement of human labor by machinery. There is no difference between a plant charge of this nature and a similar sum repaid as a "B" payment. (Douglas 1951, 42)

Clearly, Wicksell and Douglas were the exceptions. Classical, radical, neoclassical, Keynesian, New-Keynesian and New-Classical political economists ignored the underlying mechanics of exchange. The absence of empirically-consistent models of exchange, I maintain, owes, in large part, to the nature and intent of classical political economy. By the late 18th century, mercantilism was firmly entrenched in most European capitals. Among other things, mercantilism equated money with wealth. The more money (specie) a country had, the wealthier it was. The first to disagree were the French Physiocrats, according to whom, only land was capable of producing wealth. This was followed by the classical political economists in Great Britain (e.g. Adam Smith and David Ricardo), who saw large-scale manufacturing, made possible by the Watt-Boulton reciprocating steam engine, as the ultimate source of wealth.

The resulting enmity, I argue, had a profound effect on political economy. Money, and, more importantly, the exchange process itself, were, in the ensuing period, virtually ignored. Economic principles were heretofore cast in real terms. Real prices (exchange ratios) were preferred to nominal prices (prices in terms of money) (Ricardo 1817). This aversion to all things monetary extended well into the 20th century, as evidenced by the presence of the classical dichotomy, which separated the real sector from the monetary sector (Pigou 1917,1949; Hicks 1935). Arthur Pigou explains:

In the years preceding the first world war there were in common use among economists a number of metaphors, all of a like general tendency, about the role of money. "Money is a wrapper in which goods come to you"; "money is the garment draped round the body of economic life"; "money is a veil behind which the action of real economic forces is concealed". The mercantilists, it was said, in their blindness, mistook money for wealth; we must not do that.

> We must strip the garment, tear away the veil, look through the thing to the thing signified. (Pigou 1949, 18)

The Great Depression and the writings of John M. Keynes ushered in a new era. Suddenly, money took on a whole new meaning. To Keynes, the depression in the mid-1920's in Great Britain was first and foremost a monetary phenomenon, specifically, the result of an overvalued currency (i.e. the British Pound) and an inflated bank rate (Beaudreau 1999b). The problem, however, was the absence of formal models incorporating money (Clower and Howitt 2000).

In the post-World War II period, attempts were made to fill this void. Don Patinkin's *Money, Interest and Prices*, for example, was first published in 1956, followed by a series of critiques, beginning with Chris Archibald and Richard Lipsey's 1958 paper "Monetary and Value Theory: A Critique of Lange and Patinkin," followed by Robert Clower's seminal paper, "The Keynesian Counter-Revolution: A Theoretical Appraisal." published in 1967. The problems were numerous. Among the most damning was the Clower criticism, namely that in Patinkin's model, monetary exchange was altogether absent. Money entered the representative agent's utility function much like any other good. To Clower, money was synonymous with exchange. A good theory of money would, as such, require a good theory of exchange. This, as it turns out, is where the literature is today. Robert Clower continues to this day to search for the "holy grail" of monetary theory, namely a unified theory of money and markets (Howitt and Clower 2000; Clower 1995).

Like the literature it seeks to replace, this body of work suffers from a number of shortcomings. One is its ahistorical nature. No attempt is made to examine the historical development of money and markets in search of clues. Instead, as in Patinkin's early work, money and markets are modelled in a setting in which agents are specialized agglomerated geographically (Howitt 2000). In other words, trade, markets and money are not derived from first principles, namely, spatially-dispersed autarkic agents. Instead, starting with geographically-agglomerated, specialized agents, the development of markets is examined (Howitt 2000).[1]

It is felt that a more balanced approach to understanding money and markets would combine both theory and history. After all, the main objective is to explain (understand) past and present exchange technologies (producer-merchant), not some virtual exchange technology. To begin filling this void, I now turn and examine the development of various exchange technologies throughout the ages.

2.4 Exchange Throughout the Ages

In this section, I examine briefly the evolution of specialization and exchange throughout the ages, beginning with the upper Paleolithic era. The underlying motive is relatively straightforward, namely, to search for clues about the underlying nature of large-scale specialization and exchange (Beaudreau 2003). To simplify the task, I use the exchange technology taxonomy summarized in Table 2.1. There are, in general, two types of exchange, non-intermediated and intermediated, the former consisting of what amounts to spontaneous exchange/trade among economic agents, and the latter, involving specialized agents.

Non-intermediated exchange can be further broken down into simple double-coincidence of wants barter, and monetary exchange (involving a numéraire—money). Intermediated exchange is broken down into merchant-intermediated (coordinated) exchange, and producer-merchant-intermediated exchange. Merchant-intermediated exchange, as the title implies, involves exchange in the presence of a merchant who oversees the purchase and sale of commodities. Producer-merchant-intermediated exchange involves the presence of producers and merchants (distinct individuals) who oversee the purchase of factor services in the case of the producer, and output in the case of the merchant.

How did money as we know it today arise? In what conditions? Was large-scale specialization the result of money, or vice versa? Or, were these developments simultaneous? What was (were) the key factor(s)? Where and when? As it turns out, the existing literature on money and monetary theory provides little in the way of satisfactory answers to these questions. It does, however, address and answer questions such as whether a monetary equilibrium exists, and whether it was unique? Should money be in the utility function?, should money be in the production function? Is money neutral—super neutral? What is the appropriate definition of money?

Consequently, our current understanding of the origins of money is limited, not to mention limiting, and can be summarized in terms of the following parable. Consider the case of two agents, each having endowments of goods, and each having preferences defined over these goods. Assuming that the endowment does not lie in the core, it follows that trade between these two agents will be Pareto improving. Each can be made better off by exchanging some of the abundant good against the scarce good. Next, introduce a third agent, and relax the double-coincidence of wants. In this case, single pair-wise exchanges are not Pareto improving. One party is made better of, while the other is made worse off. Introducing a numéraire solves the underlying problem. Next, introduce incomplete information. Suppose that agents have either no information or limited information on trading opportunities. Again, in this case, the introduction of a numéraire would be Pareto improving. Money decreases information costs, storage costs, transport costs, etcetera.

Table 2.1
Exchange Technologies

Non-Intermediated	Intermediated
Double Coincidence of Wants	Merchant-Intermediated
Monetary Exchange	Producer-Merchant Intermediated

In short, money emerged spontaneously as a means to minimize the costs of exchange. By reducing information costs, transportation costs, and storage costs, it contributed to raising social welfare. Consider, for example, the view of money contained in Olivier Blanchard and Stanley Fischer's *Lectures on Macroeconomics*:

> Money plays two distinct roles in the economy: money is the medium of exchange, and it is usually also the unit of account. As a medium of exchange, it must be held between exchanges and thus also serves also a store of value. As a store of value, however, it is dominated by many other assets. The unit of account and medium of exchange functions of money are conceptually distinct and have sometimes been distinct in practice, especially during times of high inflation when a foreign money is, often used as unit of account while the local money continues to be used as medium of exchange. In this chapter we focus on money as a medium of exchange. Whether it is also the unit of account is of little relevance to the issues at hand. Later in the book, when we study business cycles, we will consider how both roles may combine to generate a potential role of money in business cycle fluctuations. Early monies took the form of commodities whose value in exchange was equal to their consumption value as commodities. The fact that these commodities were used as money raised their relative price. In contrast, the value of an unbacked, non-commodity money such as modern money derives only from the fact that it can be exchanged. (Blanchard and Fischer 1989, 154)

The historical—including archeological—literature on the origins of money, however, provides a widely contrasting account of the origins of money. Specifically, the historical and archeological records show that virtually all early monies were stuck by governments, be they the pharaohs, kings, or czars. According to Heather Pringle, money first appeared in ancient Mesopotamia.

> In all likelihood, human beings first being contemplating cash just about the time that Mesopotamians were slathering mortar on mud bricks to build the worlds first cities. To furnish these new temples and to serve temple officials, many farmers became artisans, stonemasons, silversmiths, tanners, weavers, boat builders, furniture makers. And within a few centuries, the cities became much greater than the sum of their parts. Economic life flourished and grew increasingly complex. Just how complex life grew in these early metropolises can be glimpsed in the world's oldest accounting records: 8,612 tiny clay tokens excavated from the floors of village houses and city temples across the Near East and studied in detail by Denise Schmand-Besserat, an archeologist at the University of Texas at Austin. The tokens served first as counters, and perhaps later as promissory notes given to tax collectors before writing appeared. (Pringle 1998, 65)

Moreover, there is no archaeological evidence of the existence of non-government monies.[2] In other words, there is no evidence that monetary exchange emerged spontaneously in an n agent environment with transactions costs (large-scale). According to numismatologist Michael Marotta:

> The theory that merchants invented coinage is widely found in authoritative works on money, banking, economics, and numismatics, as well as the history of technology. The Encyclopedia Britannica claims that the first coins bore a primitive punch mark, "certifying to either weight or fineness, or both." The ANA "Money Talks" radio series also broadcast this idea, complete with a visual sketch of Asian merchants exchanging fine wares for coins. This theory is full of holes.
>
> 1. If a merchant ever marked a lump of metal to know it again, it was to avoid taking back "the bad penny." The purpose of trade is exchange. Once you spend your coins, you never expect to see the metal again.
>
> 2. If coins were invented for trade, there would be hoards of the oldest coins all over the ancient world, clustered at trade centers. In fact, such hoards are conspicuous in their absence. The earliest known coins did not travel far from home.
>
> 3. The fact that the first coins were made of electrum leads to another problem with the commercial theory. Electrum is a naturally-occurring alloy. Electrum ranges in color and color alone is not a good indicator of alloy. So, no one could have guaranteed its fineness or "purity." It wasn't until

250 BC (400 years after coins were invented) that Archimedes discovered how to assay an alloy by measuring its specific gravity.

4.   Furthermore, no one has ever suggested a meaning to the punch marks which appear on the earliest coins. There is no known way to see in the impressions the name of a merchant or the weight of the ingot or its fineness.

5.   The Phoenicians, were among the very last, not first, ancient people to mint coins. If coinage were invented to facilitate trade, it didn't impress the greatest traders of the day. (Interesting also is that common Phoenician coins don't carry Tyrian or Sidonian art, but the symbols of the Greeks and Egyptians: An Owl with Crook and Flail.)

6.   Spending the earliest known coins would have been difficult because the first known coins were worth more than anything you could buy with them. Colin Kraay, in his book, *Archaic and Classical Greek Coins*, says "the natural assumption that coins were used in remote antiquity much as they are used today is frequently falsified by the absence of those small denominations which alone make such a use possible." (Marotta 1994, 1)

Based on the evidence found in the historical and archaeological records, money, in its current form, was not a spontaneous development involving optimizing Nash (read: private) agents, but, rather, was a product of empire building (agglomeration), which, I define as the increasing size, expanse, and reach of civil administrations (centralization). Contrary to the current view, money and the current form of exchange organized around specialized traders (producers and merchants), evolved in response to government, specifically, to the problem of public choice-induced specialization, and the resulting coordinating and exchange problems. As I shall attempt to show, without large-scale government, the current exchange technology (money and specialized traders) may not have evolved.

2.4.1 Money: An Empirically-Consistent Account

A reading of both the recent literature on money and trade in the ancient economy, and the history of the ancient and modern economy revealed a number of what I shall, for want of a better word, refer to as "regularities." These include the fact that early monies are all, without exception, specific to large political—governmental—entities. By large, it should be understood, more important than the local tribe, or groupings of local tribes. All were struck by governments/rulers. And, all coexisted with taxation of one form or another. There is no evidence, at least to my knowledge, of private monies (i.e. non-governmental) in the ancient world—in spite of the presence of specialized traders.

How can these "regularities" be explained? Part of the answer, I believe, lies with developments in the art of governing, specifically, in the art of governing large geographical expanses (e.g. Sumeria, Mesopotamia, China, Persia, Rome, etcetera). By "governing," it should be understood "public choice."

On January 25, 1695, one of my paternal ancestors, Urbain Baudereau dit Graveline, an immigrant to Canada from France, was killed in a skirmish with Iroquois warriors intent on wiping out the colony on the island of Montreal—or, at the very least, weaken it. A colonist by day, he was also a corporal in the colonial militia, ready to defend the then-young colony from attack. Contrast this with the Roman empire, and its 2,000,000 permanent troops, stationed throughout much of the Mediterranean basin, and beyond. Roman legionnaires were full-time soldiers, specialized in the art of war—or defence. Citizens of the Roman empire, regardless of their views on issues such as war and defence, consumed "military services," paid for out of government revenues, the most important source of which was taxes on its citizens.

These two cases represent opposites on the public goods spectrum. In the case of my ancestor, defence services (public good) were provided by all able-bodied citizens. There was no specialization, and hence, no need for trade. By contrast, Roman legionnaires were defence professionals (specialists) skilled in the art of war (defence). Clearly, while my ancestor could live off of the spoils of his land (autarky), Roman legionnaires depended on government (society) for their livelihood (specialization).

This brings me to the question of trade. How is trade for government services (defence, religion) in large geopolitical agglomerations carried out? How do these societies go about allocating a portion of what it produces to those who provide services to the state? Theoretically, there are a number of options. I shall focus on two, namely hierarchy and markets. I begin with hierarchy. In this case, the state, through its administrative officers, appropriates goods—and services—from its citizens in the form of a tax or levy. These are then used to remunerate the providers of public goods (armies, civil servants, government members). Provided that the government is organized efficiently (with a system of warehouses and bookkeeping), there is no reason to doubt the success of such a system.

By contrast, a society (via its government) could choose a system based on money and markets. In this case, the government issues money (bronze coins, for example), declares it legal tender, and requires that taxes be paid in it. To be more precise, the government issues coinage, uses it to purchase goods and services, and then imposes taxes and levies on its subjects, payable in its coinage (legal tender). In time, organized markets appear, complete with merchants who buy and sell goods.[3]

A system based on money, (royal) merchants and markets would have numerous advantages over one based on hierarchies (centralized). For one, governments would not have to devote scarce resources to the day-to-day operation of empire-wide exchange. More importantly, the decision of what to produce, and in what quantities, would be left to the merchant class. The problem of unused inventories would, as such, be eliminated. Another advantage is the possibility of extra-empire trade. For example, a government, by issuing new coins, could raise resources for a military strike in very little time. If its money was accepted outside of the empire, then it could benefit from increased seignorage.

History shows, quite decisively, that a system based on money, merchants and markets was preferred by most sovereigns to one based on hierarchies, and, a clear preference for sovereigns of large nation states and empires. In fact, one could go as far as to argue that money, merchants and markets were as important to the Sumerian, Persian, Chinese, Greek, and Roman empires as military acumen. It therefore follows that, notwithstanding isolated instances of money evolving spontaneously among optimizing agents (POW camps, etcetera), money as we know it today should be viewed as a creation of the state, specifically of public choice in large agglomerations. More important is the fact that money, merchants and markets were simultaneous developments, all having their origins—at least in their current form—in large political agglomerations.[4]

2.4.2 Money, Merchants, Taxes, and "Making the Market"

It is my view that an in-depth appreciation of the history of money, merchants, markets and taxes is an important input into understanding—and ultimately modelling—the process of exchange in modern societies. Take, for example, merchants. What is their role? How do they do they go about it? What are the associated risks? Historically, royal merchants were middle men, intermediating between consumers (society, government) and producers, purchasing goods from the latter, and selling them to the former, using money as the means of payment. Chief among their concerns, however, were the problems of forecasting demand, and coordinating supply. If a Roman cereal merchant overestimated the demand for wheat, then he would be left with inventories. On the other hand, if he underestimates it, then he risks losing sales, and, more importantly, losing long-standing customers—perhaps even the local government.

Given the nature of early market exchange (i.e. involving government procurement), it stands to reason that government expenditure, defined generally, was the prime determinant of merchant activity. Put differently, governments, by way of their purchases, "made the market." For example, a planned military expedition in a foreign land would no doubt lead merchants to increase their orders for military boots, clothing, and armaments. The government would use its coinage to finance the purchase of goods and services. This money would then find its way into royal and private merchants' coffers, and ultimately, into the pockets of suppliers, who would have to remit a portion of it to the government in the form of taxes. The circle would be complete. The government would have received its goods and services, the people would have received government services, and, lastly, the government would have recuperated its coinage.

It bears noting that while merchants were ultimately responsible for creating income (i.e. from the purchase of goods and services), it was government expenditure that determined the level of market-based economic activity. I refer to this as "making the market." In general, merchants did not spontaneously increase orders of goods in anticipation of greater demand on the part of private citizens—although, theoretically, they could have. The risks of doing so were too great. What if the anticipated increase in demand did not materialize? Moreover, there were strategic problems. While increasing orders from producers would increase overall income, there was no guarantee that the demand for an individual merchant's wares would increase. Put differently, an individual merchant intent on increasing purchases of, say, boots, could not count on the producers of boots (the recipients of his income—trade credit) to purchase the boots in question. As I will go on to argue, the problem of income creation (i.e. making the market) is strategic in nature, owing in large measure to the public or social nature of monetary income. If a single merchant increases orders from suppliers, then there is little chance it will succeed in selling its merchandise, for lack of buyers. However, if all merchants do so, then overall income will increase, thus increasing the chances of selling the goods in question.

This, I argue, explains the paucity of spontaneous trade in pre-industrial economies (i.e. before the 19th century). Rather, exchange in pre-industrial economies was limited, for the most part, to what I refer to as public goods, specifically government and religious services (Finley 1973; Garnsey, Hopkins and Whittaker 1983), giving rise to what I call "public choice-related trade."

2.4.3 The Emergence of Spontaneous Trade

It is fair to say that the history of trade as defined here is, for all intents and purposes, dominated by public goods and government, spontaneous trade being a relatively new phenomenon.[5] Public choice-related trade, by which it should be understood, trade involving government/religious services, is, like civilization itself, over five thousand years old.[6] The emergence of spontaneous trade, on the other hand, is a relatively recent phenomenon. This raises a number of questions, including when, why and how did spontaneous trade emerge?[7]

Spontaneous trade, I argue, was the result of a number of factors. First, there was the growing disenchantment in the 18th century with imperial governments, and, consequently, with mercantilism. Government hierarchies had grown considerably, as had their costs (government revenue). The Physiocratic movement in France, headed by Anne-Robert Jacques Turgot and Francois Quesnay, and the American Revolution bear witness to the growing disenchantment with government as the ultimate arbitrator of wealth. Second, there were technology shocks. Richard Arkwright's spinning jenny, James Watt's high-efficiency steam engine and reciprocating engine (with James Boulton) set the stage for a new form of wealth creation, namely inanimate energy-based manufacturing. These two factors, I argue, contributed to a paradigm shift in Western civilization. Wealth appropriation through trade (mercantilism) was replaced by wealth creation through manufacture (processing, adding value, value added, industry).[8]

The distinguishing feature in so far as high-throughput, continuous-flow manufacturing is concerned was its spontaneous nature—that is, independent of government. While some former royal merchants invested in manufacturing, most industrialists were non-governmental. The important point, as far as exchange technology is concerned, is that trade would never be the same. From this point on, private merchants and private producers would have to, collectively, "make the market."

Governments could no longer be counted on to "make the market." As I shall argue throughout this book, while the history of inanimate energy-based civilization is glorious, the story of producer-merchant mediated exchange is punctuated by episodes of despair and depression, based, in large measure, on the nature of the underlying game, more specifically, on the inability of private merchants and producers to "make markets" commensurately with their ability to create wealth, which, as I have argued elsewhere, is intimately tied to its use of inanimate energy (Beaudreau 1996a,1998,1999a). In the next section, I present a simple model that captures the essence of producer-merchant exchange.

2.5 A Heterodox Model of Producer-Merchant Exchange

Despite a long illustrious history, merchant exchange and producer-merchant exchange have been absent and continue to be absent from mainstream economics. In microeconomics, there is no mention whatsoever of the merchant's problem (Henderson and Quandt 1980; Varian 1992). That is, buying with the intent of reselling.[9] For roughly a century, trade has been modelled as a spontaneous activity that takes place in fictitious markets (Walrasian), guided by Adam Smith's invisible hand.

There have been exceptions, including Knut Wicksell's description of exchange in his 1898 *Interest and Prices*, Clifford H. (Major) Douglas' description of exchange in an industrial economy, and Frederich Hayek's description of exchange in his work on inflation. More recent examples of non-Walrasian-based exchange include post-Keynesian "Circuit" theories of money (Parquez and Seccareccia 2000), and Benjamin Bental and Benjamin Eden's work on uncertain and sequential trade (UST) economies (Bental and Eden 1996; Williamson 1996).

While an improvement over Walrasian models, these models fail to capture the essence of uncertain and sequential trade, namely the presence of specialized traders (coordinating agents). As my brief history of exchange has shown, merchants have, from the beginning, played an integral part in exchange—to the point of defining it. This section presents a simple model of producer-merchant exchange, which mimics the exchange process in modern industrialized economies.

2.5.1 Bankers and Banking

To begin with, I assume the existence of a single merchant banker, who, by government decree (fiat), has the right to extend credit to producers and merchants.[10] Credit notes and bills of exchange are the relevant credit instruments. For my purposes, I will assume that credit is a free good. That is, there are no costs to producers and merchants associated with using credit to finance their activities. As such, the value of the banker's assets must be identically equal to the value of his liabilities.

2.5.2 Producers and Merchants

I consider an environment in which there exist $2n$ producers and one merchant, the former transforming raw materials using capital and labor into consumption and capital goods, and the latter buying and selling these goods (transformation) at a fixed point in geographical space (shop).[11] As such, value added is assumed to be an increasing function of capital and labor.[12]

Variables

V_{ic} = consumption good producer i's value added.
V_{ik} = capital good producer i's value added.
ω_{ic} = consumption good producer i's demand for working capital.
ω_{ik} = capital good producer i's demand for working capital.
π_{ic} = consumption good producer i's profits.
π_{ik} = capital good producer i's profits.
V_c = aggregate consumption good value added.
V_k = aggregate capital good value added.
ω_c = aggregate consumption good producers' demand for working capital.
ω_k = aggregate capital good producers' demand for working capital.
ω_m = merchant demand for working capital.
π_c = aggregate consumption good producer profits.
π_k = aggregate capital good producer profits.
α = working capital's average and marginal value product.
β = consumption good overall income elasticity.

Equations

$$V_{ic} = \alpha \omega_{ic} \tag{2.1}$$

$$V_{ik} = \alpha \omega_{ik} \tag{2.2}$$

$$V_c = \alpha \omega_c \tag{2.3}$$

$$V_k = \alpha \omega_k \tag{2.4}$$

$$V_c = \sum_{i=1}^{n} V_{ic} \tag{2.5}$$

$$V_k = \sum_{i=1}^{n} V_{ik} \tag{2.6}$$

$$\omega_c = \sum_{i=1}^{n} \omega_{ic} \tag{2.7}$$

$$\omega_k = \sum_{i=1}^{n} \omega_{ik} \tag{2.8}$$

$$\omega_m = f[\omega_c + \omega_k, \pi_c + \pi_k] \tag{2.9}$$

$$\pi_{ic} = 1/n [\omega_c + \omega_k] - \omega_{ic} \tag{2.10}$$

$$\pi_c = \sum_{i=1}^{n} \pi_{ic} \tag{2.11}$$

$$\pi_{ik} = 1/n [\pi_c + \pi_k] - \omega_{ik} \tag{2.12}$$

$$\pi_k = \sum_{i=1}^{n} \pi_{ik} \tag{2.13}$$

The Exchange and Production Processes

As pointed out, exchange and production in this model is sequential in nature. Specifically, to begin with, consumption and capital good producers acquire working capital (from the bank) with which to hire the variable factor inputs, in this case, labor. The actual production functions are defined in Equations 2.1 and 2.2. Value added in both sectors is increasing in the level of working capital.[13] Working capital, in this case, is a proxy for all variable factor inputs. The aggregate levels of working capital and value added are determined by Equations 2.5 to 2.8. It is important to point out that the demand for working capital on the part of producers is less than the level of value added by an amount equal to profits. Profits, in this case, are a residual form of payment, made once output has been sold to the merchant.[14] The demand for working capital on the latter's behalf (Equation 2.9) is assumed, to begin with, to be a function of anticipated sales, which, it is argued, are a function of aggregate wage income and aggregate profit income. It is assumed that all wage income is spent on consumption goods, while all profit income is spent on capital goods. Consequently, the higher is wage income, the greater are anticipated sales of consumption goods; the higher is profit income, the greater are anticipated sales of capital goods.

As it turns out, Equation 2.9 plays a prominent role in the model. Do merchants base their demand for consumption and capital goods on actual values of macroeconomic aggregates (e.g. $\omega_c + \omega_k$, $\pi_c + \pi_k$), on past values, or on anticipated values? Clearly, if s/he overestimates demand, then goods will go unsold, inventories will build up, and losses will ensue. On the other hand, if s/he underestimates demand, then producers will be left with unsold goods.

Producer profits (consumption and capital good producers) are defined by Equations 2.10 and 2.12. We see that the representative consumption good producer's profits are, by definition, equal to its share of the merchant's working capital allocated to consumption goods, defined here as $\omega_c + \omega_k$, minus its own demand for working capital, ω_{ic}. Implicitly, it is assumed that producers maximize profits by chosing $\omega_{ic}*$, the optimal level of working capital. Equation 2.11 defines consumption goods producers aggregate profits. Equation 2.11 describes the representative capital good producer's profits. In this case, revenues are equal to each individual producer's share of aggregate profit income.

Once product markets have cleared, merchants use the proceeds to pay off the loans (working capital) they took out to finance trade. It is assumed that merchants have no costs, and, hence, earn no income (i.e. percentage of sales).[15]

Equilibrium Conditions

Equations 2.1-2.13 implicitly define a Nash game in working capital (ω) involving the $2n$ producers and the merchant. The representative consumption-good producer chooses ω_{ic}, given ω_{ic} for all other consumption good producers, for all capital good producers, and ω_m, the demand for working capital on the part of the merchant. The representative capital good producer does likewise, as does the merchant.

Equilibrium will be defined in terms of value added, working capital, and profits. Equations 2.14–2.16 define equilibrium in the consumption good, capital good, and merchant sectors of the economy. In the case of consumption good sector, equilibrium requires that the value of output be equal to the aggregate level of consumption and capital good producer working capital, producer working capital being the key determinant of the demand for consumption goods. In the case of the capital goods sector, equilibrium requires that the value of output be equal to the aggregate level of consumption and capital good producer profits. Lastly, in the case of the merchant, equilibrium requires that its overall level of working capital be equal to aggregate value added (consumption and capital goods), which, via Equation 2.16, is equal to the aggregate wage bill and aggregate profits.

$$V_c = \omega_c + \omega_k \tag{2.14}$$

$$V_k = \pi_c + \pi_k \tag{2.15}$$

$$\omega_m = V_c + V_k = \omega_c + \omega_k + \pi_c + \pi_k \tag{2.16}$$

Given the sequential nature of trade, non-zero equilibria are tenuous at best. As pointed out earlier, the nature of the game played by producers and the merchant (i.e. Nash) militates against non-zero equilibria. The reason owes to the nature of aggregate behavior. Individual producers choose ω, their working capital, given ω for all other producers, and ω_m for the merchant. Starting from an initial zero equilibrium, production and exchange cannot arise spontaneously. For non-zero output to arise, either the producers or the merchant must precommit to non-zero levels of working capital. Another possibility is in terms of expectations. If sufficiently many producers expect non-zero ω_m, then non-zero equilibria can arise. Similarly, if the merchant expects that producers will produce non-zero levels of output, then non-zero equilibria can arise.

2.5.3 The Demand for Money

The demand for money in a producer-merchant model of an exchange economy differs from conventional models in a number of important ways (Laidler 1977,1990). First, two sets of agents demand money (working capital, credit), namely producers who coordinate production, and the merchant (merchants) who coordinates distribution. Producers demand working capital (money) in order to transact in factor markets (i.e. acquire variable inputs). Formally, this is captured by Equations 2.17-2.18 which are obtained by inverting Equations 2.1 and 2.2. As such, ($1/\alpha$) should as such be seen as the demand for credit per dollar of value added. For example, if α takes on the value of 1.4285, then the value-added elasticity of the demand for credit is 0.70. As for the merchant, s/he demands working capital to finance the purchase of goods (rolling stock). This is captured by Equation 2.19 above.

$$\omega_{ic} = (1/\alpha) V_{ic} \tag{2.17}$$

$$\omega_{ik} = (1/\alpha) V_{ik} \tag{2.18}$$

From this, it follows that the elasticity of the overall demand for money per unit of value added exceeds unity. That is, for V_{ic} of value added (consumption and capital good), the demand for money is $\omega_{ic} + V_{ic}$ This reflects the fact that value added undergoes two transformations, namely its initial transformation (producer) and its secondary transformation (merchant). It should be pointed out, however, that, at any one point in time, the demand for credit can never be greater than the amount of the value added.

Relationship to the Demand for Money Literature

This view of the demand for money differs in many ways from the standard view found in the literature (Laidler 1977,1993). In conventional models, the demand for money on the part of agents is an increasing function of income, and a decreasing function of the opportunity cost of holding cash balances. Here, it is modelled as an increasing function of consumption and capital goods producers' and the merchant's demand for working capital. This, I maintain, captures more accurately the integral role of producers and merchants in the demand for money.

It should, however, be pointed out that while it is somewhat orthogonal to the existing literature, it does, nonetheless, address a number of criticisms levelled, over the course of the past century, at work on the demand for money literature. Consider, for example, Harold Moulton's remarks regarding "Money in Relation to Production."

> When money is spoken of as a medium of exchange, one usually has in mind the exchange of consumer goods. For convenience of exposition, economic treatises have commonly been divided into four parts, devoted respectively to consumption, production, exchange, and distribution. Money is treated under exchange and its chief function is usually regarded as that of effecting the exchange of goods that have already been produced and are in the market awaiting transfer to the hands of those who are to consume them. But if one is to appreciate fully the significance of money under a capitalistic industrial regime, it is necessary to consider the part that it plays in the productive as well as in the exchange process. Exchange of consumers' goods is not to be excluded; but the role of money in getting goods ready to be exchanged as completed products must be included. Modern business is almost universally conducted through the use of money. With money the manufacture purchases the materials needed for the construction of his plant; with money he employs an administrative staff to manage his business; and with money he purchases the raw materials and supplies and employs the labor force required to operate his business. In a similar way producers of raw materials, transportation agencies, and wholesalers and retailers employ money in connection with every other phase of their business operations; under modern conditions even the farmer makes an extensive use of money. In short, practically the entire production process is nowadays organized and operated through the use of

money… Because of the great importance that has always been attached to money as capital, the economist has been wise in laying emphasis upon the fact that real capital consists of tangible properties. However, this emphasis has in turn tended to minimize the significant part that money plays in a capitalistic society. Productive instruments cannot be made effective in the service of society unless liquid capital is available with which to assemble raw materials and labor power in producing organizations. (Moulton 1938, 21)

A similar critique is found in Williford I. King's 1920 *American Economic Review* article entitled "Circulating Capital: Its Nature and Relation to the Public Welfare:"

Despite the fact that bank notes or deposits are used in the daily business of hundreds of millions of people, there still remain numerous misconceptions concerning the nature of these media of exchange. Furthermore, it seems safe to assert that few indeed, not only the users but also of the bankers who issue the obligations, have any clear idea of just what effects upon the public such issues produce. According to the writers observation, textbooks in economics rarely touch upon this last and most important phase of the problem. It therefore appears to be worth while to discuss in some detail the fundamental principles connected with bank credit. Bank credit is used mainly for business purposes. Some loans from banks are obtained in order to purchase consumption goods, but loans for this purpose form so small a fraction of the total that they scarcely need consideration here. The bulk of credit loaned, not only by banks, but by other lenders as well, is nowadays borrowed for purposes of investment or the use in the undertakings for profit making. (King 1920, 738)

The producer-merchant model of exchange, I submit, addresses these concerns, and, moreover, provides an empirically-consistent model of the exchange process in industrial economies. Whereas in traditional analysis, the demand for money is modelled as an increasing function of aggregate income, here it is modelled as the outcome of optimizing individual producers and merchants.

2.5.4 A Numerical Example

Consider the following numerical example. Suppose to begin with that each of the two sectors consists of 10 producers, that consumption-good producers each produce $7.00 of value added ($V_{ic}$), that capital-good producers each produce $3.00 of value added ($V_{ik}$), and that α and β assume values of 1.428 and 0.7 respectively. Accordingly, consumption-good producers require $4.90 of credit to finance variable costs (ω_{ic}), while capital-good producers require $2.10 of credit to finance variable costs (ω_{ik}). The total demand for credit on the part of consumption-goods producers is $49.00 ($\omega_c$); the total demand for credit on the part of capital-goods producers is $21.00 ($\omega_k$). Total value added by consumption-goods producers is $70.00 ($V_c$); total value added by capital-goods producers is $30.00 ($V_k$).

Aggregate value added is $100.00. The merchant requires $100.00 of credit ($\omega_m = V_c + V_k$), with which to finance the purchase of consumption and capital goods. The aggregate demand for consumption goods is $70.00, while the aggregate demand for capital goods is $30.00. The relevant sequence of events (trades) is as follows. Producers demand credit with which to finance output; the merchant then demands consumption and capital goods, financing their acquisition with credit. Consumption-good producers earn $2.1 of profit each ($\pi_{ic}$), while capital-good producers earn $0.9 of profit ($\pi_{ik}$), the sum of which goes to the acquisition of capital goods. Merchants use the proceeds from the sale of consumption and capital goods to retire the outstanding bank liability ($100.00).

2.5.5 Making Goods and Making Markets

This simple model of exchange makes a key, fundamental, and, until now, over-looked point about producers, namely that in addition to making goods and services, producers "make markets" via their transactions in factor markets. By increasing their demand for labor, they increase overall income, thus contributing to the activity that I refer to as "making of the market" (aggregate income). The corollary, it therefore follows, is what I refer to as "unmaking the market," which consists of reducing the demand for labor, and, as such, reducing overall income. This two aspects of producer behavior are often ignored. Another overlooked aspect is the orthogonal nature of producers' factor market behavior and their product market behavior. Put differently, the income producers generate (via ω_{ic}) will, in most cases, have little-to-no bearing on their sales, and hence revenue. In the model, a one dollar increase in operating capital will increase the representative consumption good producer's sales by $1/n$ dollar. As n increases, this share decreases, going to zero in the limit.

Perhaps this explains why it is common practice today to view the market (aggregate income-working capital) as being independent of producer costs. As such, decisions that affect the cost side of the ledger (working capital) are rarely seen as having an impact on the revenue side of the ledger. However, while this may hold true at the individual producer level, it does not hold true at the aggregate level, where aggregate producer behavior affects aggregate income, which affects aggregate merchant behavior, and so on and so forth.

2.5.5 Sequential Exchange, Uncertainty and Expectations

Given the sequential nature of trade, it stands to reason that consumption and capital goods producers' decisions in factor markets will be predicated on their expectations regarding the overall economic activity, and, more specifically, the demand for their product(s). An anticipated increase in overall economic activity will increase producer demand for operating capital, and, hence, for value added. Similarly, the merchants' decisions in product markets (consumption and capital goods) will be predicated on their expectations regarding producer behavior as well as on aggregate merchant behavior.

This highlights the game-theoretical (read: strategic) nature of what could be referred to as the "making the market" game. Producers base their decisions on their expectations of what their fellow producers and merchants will do. The result is a class of expectational Nash equilibria. This section examines these equilibria in more detail.

Expectations

Let:

$[\omega_m]_{ic=}^e$ consumption good producer i's expectation of the overall level of merchant income.

$[\omega_m]_{ik=}^e$ capital good producer i's expectation of the overall level of merchant income.

$V_c^e =$ the merchant's expectation of the overall level of consumption good output.

$V_k^e =$ the merchant's expectation of the overall level of capital good output.

As one can clearly see, the problem of expectational equilibria is multi-dimensional. In the model, all $2n$ producers and the merchant are assumed to form their own expectations, which may or may not be identical. Just how they go about forming expectations, however, is beyond the scope of the present work.

Suffice it to say that there are as many "expectational" equilibria as there are combinations of producer and merchant expectations.

To further understand the role of expectations in the model, I examine various expectational equilibria. To this end, I assume that producers' and merchants' expectations are either (1) bullish, (2) bearish, or (3) status quo. This gives rise to a total of nine possible states of nature. These are shown in Table 2.2, along with the resulting macroeconomic outcomes.

As Table 2.2 shows, the model generates a number of expectational Nash equilibrium (Farmer 1996). These are sometimes referred to as "self-fulfilling prophecies." Consider the following example. Starting from an initial equilibrium, suppose that, for some reason, producers suddenly become bearish over the future, specifically, over the level of aggregate demand (i.e. ω).[16] Acting on these expectations, they then proceed to decrease their demand for labor, and, consequently, the demand and supply of working capital. Merchants respond by decreasing planned orders of consumption and capital goods. As this case illustrates, expectations are self-fulfilling: the prophecy of lower sales "self-fulfills" itself. Producers expect lower sales, act accordingly, and, in the end, see their expectations fulfilled. The reverse situation also holds. In this case, bullish producers increase the overall demand for working capital, labor and capital. Merchants respond by increasing orders for consumption and capital goods, resulting in an increase in the level of overall output. As these examples clearly illustrate, a necessary condition for an expectational equilibrium is the presence of "passive" merchants. Specifically, in both of these cases, merchants simply validated producers' expectations, decreasing orders in bearish markets, and increasing orders in bullish markets. Consider the case, however, where merchant expectations are independent of producers expectations. Could expectations be self-fulfilling as was the case above? As it turns out, there are a number of such possibilities, illustrated in Table 2.2. If producers and merchants are bearish, then the outcome will be bearish, for obvious reasons. If producers are bearish, but merchants are neutral (status quo) (order last period's quantities), then there is a good chance that the outcome will be the status quo. The reason is straightforward, namely that merchants' orders do not decrease, prompting producers to revise their expectations upwards. If producers are bullish, and merchants are bearish, then there is a good chance that overall output and income will increase. In this case, producers', by increasing the demand for factor inputs, increase overall factor income, prompting merchants to revise their expectations upwards, thus leading, at least conceivable, to an increase in overall output and income.[17]

Table 2.2
Expectational Equilibria

Producer\Merchant	Bearish	Status Quo	Bullish
Bearish	Fall in Output	Excess Demand (P)	Excess Demand (P)
Status Quo	Excess Supply (P)	Status Quo	Excess Demand (M)
Bullish	Excess Supply (P)	Excess Supply (P)	Increase in Output

Inventories

This raises a number of questions. For example, how are these equilibria affected by the presence of inventories? Thus far, we have ignored inventories. We know, however, that both merchants and producers carry (hold) them. As it turns out, inventories have a stabilizing effect on the level of aggregate economic activity. To see this, consider the off-diagonal terms in Table 2.2. In the case in which producers are bearish and merchants are bullish, an excess demand for consumer and capital goods results as merchants increase their supplies. If producers do not hold inventories, then there arises the possibility that merchants may turn bearish on the future, and, seeing that producers are actually decreasing their output, revise their orders. The presence of inventories, however, allows merchants to realize their objectives. Thus, in lieu of signalling their desire for more consumption and capital goods via back orders, they do so via sales.

There is also the question of intra-cohort expectations. If individual consumption good producers hold inventories, then they can hedge against a bad outcome. For example, if merchants are bullish and other producers are bullish, then a bearish consumption good producer, by holding inventories, can minimize the costs of erring (expectation-wise), so to speak.

2.6 A Model of Producer-Merchant Exchange with Technology Shocks

This simple framework provides an empirically-consistent model of exchange in an advanced industrial setting. It highlights the important role played by merchants, both individually and collectively, in determining the overall level of output, employment and income. In general, merchants have been absent from macroeconomic—and microeconomic—models. In this section, I examine the properties of the resulting equilibria, specifically with regard to perturbations (shocks).

Suppose that the hypothetical economy described above is hit by an output-increasing Hicks-neutral technology shock. That is, existing labor and capital are now τ percent more productive. The relevant question is whether it can successfully make the transition to a higher equilibrium growth path in response to such a shock?[18] If so, how? If not, why not? I show that owing to the nature of the game played by profit-maximizing producers, and the fact that profits are a residual form of income, an economy consisting of $2n$ producers and a merchant playing Nash strategies, cannot make a nominal transition to the higher equilibrium growth path. I refer to the resulting equilibrium as one of income inertia, or, quite simply, underincome. Individual producers have no private incentives to increase wages, and hence, working capital. In light of this, merchants have no private incentives to increase orders of consumption and capital goods. Paradoxically, the economy suffers from inertia, in spite of improved fundamentals.

2.6.1 Private Incentives

To demonstrate this, consider Equations 2.10 and 2.12 which describe the individual producer's optimization problem. In a Nash setting (ceteris paribus), increasing one's wage τ percent—in keeping with labor productivity—will increase the producer's overall costs by more than it will increase its revenue. This is shown via Equations 2.19–2.20, where for all values of β/n and $(1-\beta)/n$ less than 1, $d\pi_{ic}$ is less than zero.

Proposition 1: In a Nash wage setting producer-merchant environment, there are no private incentives for producers to increase working capital (income) in response to a capacity-increasing technology shock.

Proposition 2: In a Nash wage-setting producer-merchant environment, working capital (income) fails to rise commensurately with a generalized capacity-increasing technology shock.

Proof:

These can be reduced to:

$$d\pi_{ic} = 1/n\,[\beta d\omega_{ic}] - d\omega_{ic} \tag{2.19}$$

$$d\pi_{ik} = 1/n\,[(1\text{-}\beta)d\omega_{ik}] - d\omega_{ic} \tag{2.20}$$

For all values of β/n less than 1, and values of $(1\text{-}\beta)/n$ less than one, $d\pi_{ic}$ and $d\pi_{ik}$ are less than zero, respectively. As 2.19 and 2.20 hold for all producers, it follows that private producers have no incentive to increase working capital, which, implies that, in the aggregate, economy-wide working capital will fail to increase commensurately with overall productive capacity. *QED*

In other words, *ceteris paribus*, increasing working capital—wages—decreases producer profits. The optimal response, as far as the individual producer is concerned, is to not increase one's wage. The resulting Nash equilibrium, it therefore follows, is characterized by what I refer to as income inertia.[19] Income inertia can also be viewed as an income and output indeterminacy. Given the nature of the game (Nash), there are no private incentives to act, resulting in collective inertia.

This raises a number of counterfactual questions. For example, could expectations overcome the inertia (underincome)? Could bullish merchants, by increasing orders of consumption and capital goods, push the economy on to the higher growth path? Theoretically, if a hypothetical bullish merchant increased orders by τ percent, then, in the short-run at least, the economy would operate at capacity. Producers would increase shipments to the merchant by τ percent. Assuming that wage rates remain constant, consumption and capital goods producers would earn windfall profits.[20] Unfortunately, this would not be sustainable in the long run as a glut of consumption—and ultimately capital—goods would appear. The τ percent more consumption goods would go unsold, which, in the medium-to-long term would lead producers to decrease their demand for capital goods, thus aborting eventually a merchant-led transition.

2.6.2 Technology Shock: A Numerical Example

Consider the numerical example presented earlier, and assume that τ assumes a value of 0.10, or 10 percent. In this case, both consumption- and capital-good producers see their productivity increase by 10 percent. At issue is the question of making the market. More specifically, who will "make the market" for the additional $10.00 worth of value added? Clearly, despite the fact that labor in both sectors is 10 percent more productive, there are no private incentives to increase wages (variable costs). In fact, increasing wages by 10 percent is profit decreasing.

Such an increase raises costs by $0.49, but only increases revenues by only $0.0343 ($0.49x0.7÷10). Clearly, there are no private incentives to increase wages and "make the market."

2.6.3 Rationalization

Thus far, we have established that there are no private incentives for producers to increase their demand for working capital (wages) in response to the technology shock. The next question is whether this is the best they can do? For example, could they do better by reducing their demand for working capital? Remember, production processes are now τ percent more productive.

As it turns out, it can easily be shown that by reducing working capital by τ percent, profits will increase. The reason has to do with the fact that each productive factor is now τ percent more productive. Producers can now fill their orders (from merchants) with τ percent fewer factor inputs. I refer to such a strategy as rationalization. I argue that, in general, rationalization and underincome go hand-in-hand, with causality running from the latter to the former. Paradoxically, higher productivity leads to lower employment.

Theoretically, at least, rationalization, at the aggregate level, can lead the producer-merchant economy described here into a downward spiral, for obvious reasons. If all producers cut working capital (employment) by τ percent, then ω_c and ω_k will fall by τ percent, thus leading merchants to decrease their orders for consumption and capital goods by τ percent, setting off a second round of layoffs. Where the ensuing downward spiral ends will depend on the underlying production technology. If there are technological limits to cutting employment (fixed labor input), then it follows that only when these limits are reached will the spiral end. If the technology is strictly linear, however, the equilibrium will be the null set.

2.7 Real Transitions

The model developed in this chapter assumes fixed prices (wages and product prices). Quantities both of consumption and capital goods, and labor—not to mention energy and intermediate inputs—increase and/or decrease, with prices remaining constant. It therefore follows that the problem of underincome as modelled here is essentially a nominal phenomenon, that is, one in which product prices, specifically product-price adjustment, have no role to play. As prices are variable, the question of product-price adjustment arises. For example, could product-price adjustment (downward) increase real income, and in the process, pave the way for a real transition to the growth path? Specifically, falling product prices, by increasing real wages (operating income divided by prices), increase the demand for consumption and capital goods, prompting merchants to increase orders from producers, thus resulting in a successful transition. In this case, while nominal income, measured by aggregate working capital, would remain constant, real income would increase by τ percent.

Among the key issues, as far as real transitions are concerned, is the question of downward price adjustment in the presence of technological change—specifically, will producers, finding themselves with τ percent more capacity, decrease product price by an equivalent amount, assuming of course that the τ is a free-good?[21] The answer is by no means obvious. First, if producer ic decreases his/her price by τ percent, then s/he runs the risk of incurring loses should demand does not increase by at least τ percent. In other words, without a guarantee that demand will increase by, at the very least, τ percent, producer ic will resist decreasing price. However, if s/he goes ahead and does reduce price, then pressure will mount to decrease operating costs, specifically labor costs, prompting calls for wage decreases.

Another important issue is the producer-merchant relationship. Specifically, will the merchant agree to reduce the sticker price of producer ic's good, in the presence of mark-up pricing. That is, if the merchant operates on a mark-up basis, s/he may be reluctant to decrease price, as it would decrease his/her revenues. Another merchant-related issue is the question of shelf space. Will the merchant increase producer ic's shelf space at the expense of competitors? This raises the strategic aspects of price decreases. How will competitors react? Will they stand pat, and watch their market share diminish? Will they react? Will possible reprisals act as a deterrent?

This raises the possibility of price-related coordination failures. In so far as producer ic is concerned, a price decrease—by τ percent—will be tolerated so long as all other producers (consumption and capital good) decrease their prices by an equivalent amount. Real profits will increase by τ percent. On the other hand, if s/he is the only one to act (i.e. decrease price), then there may be some reluctance. First, there is the question of own-price elasticity. Will demand increase sufficiently to increase profits? Will merchants stock more of his/her product at the expense of rivals? Will rivals stand pat? If all producers cut prices, will they be better off? Clearly, in a world of incomplete information, coordination failures are not only possible, but highly probable. Individually, producers will be reluctant to decrease prices, not knowing what his/her rivals will do, let alone all other $2n$-1 producers.

2.7.1 Who Makes the Market?

As I have attempted to demonstrate, the presence of productive capacity is not a sufficient condition for wealth, as classical and neoclassical writers believed. Say's Law, as such, is valid in equilibrium, but not valid out of equilibrium. Nominal and real coordination failures, as has been shown here, preclude transitions to higher equilibrium growth paths in response to technological change.

This raises the ultimate question, as far as dynamic macroeconomics is concerned, namely that in periods of technological change, who "makes the market?" Who increases nominal/real income commensurately with productive capacity? Is it individual producers who, in Benthamian and Smithian fashion, by looking out for their own good, contribute to the good of society? The results presented above suggest that owing to the nature of the game (wage and price) played by producers, private Nash economies cannot make the transition to new equilibrium growth paths. Individual producers have no private incentives to increase nominal income. Increasing nominal income in line with productivity, *ceteris paribus*, is a profit-decreasing strategy. Decreasing product price, as pointed out above, can also be a profit-decreasing strategy.

In short, while producers make the market in equilibrium, no one (merchant or producer) stands prepared to make the market out of equilibrium. The result is a classical prisoner's dilemma, where cooperative strategies are dominated by non-cooperative ones, where cooperative behavior is dominated by non-cooperative behavior.

The result is a class of paradoxical equilibria. For example, income, supply and demand could be nil in spite of positive, system-wide capacity, for lack of a merchant, for lack of income, or for lack of optimistic expectations. Technological change, it therefore follows, need not necessarily result in increased wealth and prosperity, as pointed out by Sturgeon Bell.

2.8 Policy Measures

As I have shown, profit-maximizing producers have no private interest to increase wages (working capital) in response to a Hicks-neutral technology shock. Likewise, profit-maximizing merchants have no interest to increase orders of consumption and capital goods, given the absence of higher wages (aggregate working capital). The result is underincome and inertia. The relevant question then is, can anything be done? Can the inertia be reversed? If so, then how? Here, I examine briefly some of the measures which could, at least theoretically, solve the problem of underincome. These include (1) commercial policy (2) government expenditure (3) government-based wage and price setting.

Before examining these, it is important to highlight the public-good aspects of markets, as defined in this chapter. From the producer's point of view, the market is a public good. When a producer hires a worker, s/he creates income (working capital) which benefits all producers and merchants. There is, for lack of a better word, a "market externality." Producers that reduce working capital can, as such, be viewed as free-riders in the public-good sense of the term. That is, they free-ride off of the "markets" made by others.

2.8.1 Commercial Policy

Underincome, as argued earlier, results from the presence of income inertia on the part of producers. At the individual producer level, potential wealth (value added) increases; however producer working capital does not. As aggregate producer working capital (ω_m) can, by definition, be no greater than the sum of individual producer working capital, inertia characterizes the economy as a whole. This raises the question of policy measures. What policy measures, if any, can be taken to resolve the inertia?

One possible way to correct the problem without increasing national producer working capital (ω_c, ω_k) is to turn to foreign markets. Foreign markets (nominal income), created in large measure by the factor market decisions of foreign producers, offer the possibility of increased sales and, consequently, increased profits to domestic producers. Liberalizing trade, it therefore follows, could, at least conceivably, provide domestic producers with the spectre of higher sales and higher profits.

The downside, however, is the reciprocal nature of trade liberalization. Typically, access to foreign markets is obtained in return for access to domestic markets. Foreign merchant orders from domestic producers will increase as will domestic merchants orders from foreign producers. Free trade, it therefore follows, will only be beneficial if the resulting exports exceed imports.[22]

In this case, the domestic country would either run a current account surplus, or increase any existing surplus. To this end, either domestic or foreign merchants would have to extend credit to foreign buyers. That is, domestic producers would have to accept foreign credit-based assets in return for their goods.[23] At the aggregate level, the country would run a current-account surplus and a capital-account deficit.

Conceptually at least, commercial policy is analogous to third-party intervention. The $2n$ Nash wage and price-setting producers that comprise the economy cannot, when behaving optimally, move to the new growth path. A third party is needed, which, in this case, is the foreign merchant, trading goods against foreign liabilities.

2.8.2 Government Expenditure

For traditionally-defined government expenditure to resolve the problem of income-inertia (underincome), the government must do more than tax, borrow and spend, for obvious reasons. Taxing, borrowing and spending does not increase the overall level of income; instead, it merely redistributes it. As such, traditional Keynesian-style macroeconomic policies will be ineffective. For government expenditure to be successful, the government, like the merchant, must increase the overall level of working capital (ω_m); otherwise, the problem will remain whole.

The key, it therefore follows, lies in increasing the overall level of money income. As the government cannot set wages and prices, it stands to reason that it has no choice but to increase its liabilities. Consider the following example. Suppose that the consumption good/capital good split is 70-30. That is, 70 percent of national income is in the form of consumption goods, while 30 percent is in the form of capital goods. Also suppose that national income is $100.00, and that τ assumes a value of 0.05.

In this case, the government would borrow $3.50 from the private banking system with the intention of purchasing an equivalent amount of consumption goods. The merchant would then increase orders for consumption and capital goods by 5 percent. The government would then purchase $3.50 worth of consumption goods. As a result, consumption goods producers would see their profits rise by an equivalent amount. The government would then tax 70 percent of $3.50 ($2.45), leaving $1.05 in the form of increased consumption good producer profits. The latter would then be reinvested in capital equipment (purchased at the merchant).

In turn, capital goods producers revenues and profits would rise by an equivalent amount. Overall sales would rise by $1.50, of which 70 percent would be taxed away ($1.05), leaving $0.45 in profits for capital goods producers. Remember, the merchant increases orders from consumption good and capital good producers by 5 percent. Sales of capital goods would increase by $1.05 (from consumption good producers) and $0.45 from capital good producers (own reinvestment).

Together with the proceeds from the taxation of consumption goods producers ($2.45), total tax receipts would be $3.50, the amount of the original loan (government liability). The government could, at least potentially, retire its outstanding bank liability. What is important to remember in this case, however, is the recurrent nature of government intervention. Year in and year out, government would be called upon to purchase $3.50 worth of consumption goods. The associated government debt—with private banks—would never be retired. In essence, these two cases represent a return of sorts to pre-industrial trade where, as pointed out earlier in this chapter, the government "made the market."

2.8.3 Wage and Price Policy

A fully-informed government, aware of the problem of underincome and the subtleties of the prisoner's dilemma (*Proposition 2*), could, by setting wages and prices, engineer a successful transition to the new, higher equilibrium growth path. This would be achieved either by wage policy, price policy, or some combination thereof. In the above example, a government, by legislating a τ percent, across-the-board increase in wages (operating capital), in combination with a price freeze, could solve the underlying prisoner's dilemma. As such, ω_c and ω_k would increase by τ percent, increasing the demand for merchant credit by an equivalent amount, etcetera. These increases would then work their way through the economy, resulting in an across-the-board increase in economic magnitudes of τ percent, making for a successful transition to the new, higher equilibrium growth path.

Conversely, it could opt for a real transition. For example, it could legislate a τ percent across-the-board decrease in product prices in combination with a wage freeze. In this case, real wages would increase by τ percent, thus prompting the merchant to increase orders for consumption and capital goods by τ percent. As a result, real wages and real profits would increase by τ percent, as would the overall level of economic activity, thus ensuring a successful transition to the new growth path. Finally, it could choose to combine nominal wage increases with price decreases. In this case, the sum of wage increase, measured in percent, and the negative of the price decrease, also measured in percentage, ought to be equal to τ.

2.9 Summary

This chapter set out to formalize the problem of underincome as defined in my earlier work on the Great Depression. Existing models of exchange were rejected in favor of a simple, sequential producer-merchant model that mimics the exchange technology found in western industrialized democracies. Underincome (income inertia) was derived as an equilibrium to a Nash wage game on the part of producers. The sub-optimality of the resulting equilibrium led to a discussion of policy measures, including commercial policy and government expenditure. These results will now be used to examine two types of underincome, namely, energy deepening-based underincome, and nonenergy deepening-based underincome. The former refers to underincome that results from energy deepening, defined as an increase in the consumption of energy per period of time. The latter refers to underincome that results from organization-related technology shocks. Included among these is the recent trend towards workerless factories, where animate human supervision is replaced by inanimate computer-based supervision.

Appendix: The Spontaneous Private Market Impossibility Theorem

In this chapter, it has been shown that, owing to the absence of private incentives to increase working capital (ω) in response to an economy-wide capacity-increasing technology shock, a private Nash producer-merchant economy cannot make the transition to the new higher equilibrium growth path corresponding to this technological shock. Put differently, starting from a point along a given aggregate value added growth path, private Nash economies cannot move to higher growth paths in response to a technology shock.

In this appendix, I generalize this result to all forms of intermediated exchange. Intermediated exchange differs from nonintermediated exchange by the presence of specialized traders in the former, and their absence in the latter. Nonintermediated exchange refers to exchange technologies without traders (specialized agents). Barter and primitive monetary exchange are examples. In the latter, an exchange medium (e.g. gold, silver, salt) exists, and is used in trade (see Table 2.1). Here, I show that intermediated forms of exchange cannot be supported as Nash equilibria, and hence, are unlikely to arise spontaneously. This has important implications for the history of monetary exchange. Specifically, it casts considerable doubt on the possibility of spontaneous emergence of markets and money.

Consider the simplest case of n producers (agents), each producing one unit of a differentiated good. Also assume, following Howitt and Clower (2000) that barter is too costly, and hence, not feasible. In light of this, the only way in which trade can emerge is via specialized traders (merchants), who buy and sell goods. Assume, for the sake of argument, that a specialized trader deals in only one good, and makes payment in gold (stock). Further, assume that the relative price of each of the goods is unity. The question is whether, in a Nash setting, market exchange involving specialized traders will emerge spontaneously, that is without the presence of a third party (government, coordinating agent, etcetera).

Consider, to begin with, the no-trade case. That is, there are no specialized traders. The question is, will trade (intermediated) emerge? Let us examine the potential specialized trader's problem. To enter the market (so to speak), s/he must purchase a unit of good i, and pay for it in terms of gold. The problem, however, arises on the revenue side. If s/he is the only trader, then there is little chance of selling good i, for lack of income (in this case, gold). The producer of good i has no interest in buying it back. Thus, in a Nash setting, there are no incentives to "make a market," so to speak. I refer to this result as the Spontaneous Private Market Impossibility Theorem." If spontaneous market trade is impossible, then it is unclear whether specialization will emerge. Put differently, if agents cannot sell and buy in organized markets, then there will be no incentive to specialize.

It follows that only if at least two potential specialized traders can communicate and, as a result, coordinate their activities can markets as defined here emerge. The emergence of markets is analogous to a prisoner's dilemma. Without coordination, markets organized around specialized traders cannot emerge. Examples of successful coordination in the past include the presence of public choice mechanisms (i.e. government expenditure), which, as shown earlier in this chapter, "makes the market," thus circumventing the prisoner's dilemma.

The Spontaneous Private Market Impossibility Theorem, I maintain, can be used to explain the absence of non-government market activity organized around specialized traders, and private money, in antiquity and in the pre-industrial revolution period—the Polanyi hypothesis. Making the market, by which is meant trading gold for goods with an eye to resale, is a public good. The gold (money, credit) received by the vendor (producer) is a public good as soon as s/he begins to spend it. The vendor cannot appropriate all of it for him/herself. As with all public goods, there is the risk of undersupply.

Appendix II: A Descriptive Account of Royal Merchant Trade

This appendix presents a brief descriptive account of royal merchant trade, which, as I argue, marks the beginning of markets, money and organized (inter-mediated) trade. Consider an environment in which there are *n* producers, one merchant, and one sovereign. Suppose that owing to the presence of belligerent tribes on the border of the kingdom, the sovereign must maintain a standing army, prepared at all times to defend his subjects—and his property. Suppose also that the total product of the kingdom is 100 *roi*'s, *roi*'s being the unit of account, and that the cost of a standing army is 10 *roi*'s.

As pointed out earlier, the sovereign has two choices. Either he collect 10 *roi*'s worth of output with which to pay his army in kind, or establish a system of money, merchants and taxes (monetary). If he opts for the former, then he incurs the cost of a bureaucracy, whose purpose is to collect, store, and transport the 10 *roi*'s of goods and services needed to defend the kingdom. If he chooses the latter, then he issues currency (coinage) in the amount of 10 *roi*'s, which is declared legal tender, and is paid to the army. The soldiers use the money to purchase goods and service. Furthermore, it is decreed that all taxes must, heretofore, be paid in *roi*'s. Taxpayers, in turn, must sell goods and services to the soldiers, or sell goods and services to those who sold goods and services to soldiers, etcetera. In all likelihood, specialized merchants will spontaneously arise, purchasing goods and services from individuals and paying in money (i.e. *roi*'s).

More importantly, as taxes are now payable in *roi*'s, it stands to reason that the initial 10 *roi*'s worth of trade will engender, via a multiplier-like process, more monetary trade, as citizens not dealing directly with the sovereign (or his mer-chants) will have to somehow acquire *roi*'s with which to honor their outstanding tax liability. Should the economy not be producing at capacity, one could argue that such expenditure would increase wealth. Perhaps similar considerations were what prompted mercantilists to argue that wealth was increasing in bullion.

3

Energy Deepening-Based Underincome

*It must be admitted that scientific or artificial aid to man increases his pro-
ductive powers, his natural wants remaining the same; and in proportion as
his productive powers increase he becomes less dependent on his physical
strength and on the many contingencies connected with it... That the direct
effect of every addition to scientific, or mechanical and chemical power is to
increase wealth; and it is found, accordingly, that the immediate cause of the
present want of employment from the working classes is an excess of production of all kinds of wealth, by which, under the existing arrangements of
commerce, all the markets of the world are overstocked.*

—Robert Owen, *A Report to the County of Lanark*

3.1 Introduction

In this chapter—and the next—I examine the various causes of underincome,
drawing extensively on the historical record. Recall that underincome per se is a
dynamic phenomenon that arises in the presence of paradigm technology shocks.
I begin by defining two types of shocks, namely energy deepening-based shocks
and nonenergy-deepening-based shocks. The steam engine and electrification are
examples of energy deepening-based shocks, while the ICT revolution is an
example of non-energy deepening-based technology shocks. All three can, at least
potentially, open up a gap between potential and actual GNP.

Owing to the absence of both energy and information from standard neo-clas-
sical production theory, the discussion of both energy deepening-based shocks

and non-energy deepening-based shocks will draw on earlier work on alternative models of production, notably on the energy-organization model of production developed in Beaudreau (1998), and applied in Beaudreau (1999a).

3.2 The Energy-Organization Framework

To better understand energy deepening-based and nonenergy deepening-based underincome, consider Equation 3.1, which describes the Energy-Organization approach to production developed in Beaudreau (1998). Here, $W_{ic}(t)$ is defined as the level of work in consumption good producer ic in period t, η as the level of second law efficiency, $S_{ic}(t)$, as the level of supervision in consumption good producer ic in period t, $T_{ic}(t)$ as the level of tools in consumption good producer ic in period t, and $E_{ic}(t)$ as the level of energy input in consumption good producer ic in period t. Work in this case is synonymous with the notion of transformation. In keeping with the laws of classical mechanics and thermodynamics, work is increasing in energy use (exergy). Supervision (conventionally-defined labor) and tools are not productive in the physical sense; instead, they define the framework in which energy (force) transforms nature's abundant supply of natural resources into useful, and hence, valuable, goods. Better supervision, and better tools, it follows, lead to increased second-law efficiency (i.e. η) and, hence, increased output for given $E_{ic}(t)$.[1]

$$W_{ic}(t) = \eta[S_{ic}(t), T_{ic}(t)]\, E_{ic}(t) \qquad (3.1)$$

Energy deepening-based and nonenergy deepening-based technology shocks affect the value added-based production functions via the α coefficient in Equations 3.2 and 3.3. For example, for a given ω_{ic}, energy deepening will increase V_{ic}, the level of consumption good value added for a given ω_{ic} via a higher α value. Nonenergy deepening-based shocks such as automation have an analogous effect. For example, by replacing human supervision by a control device, the same level of output (V_{ic}) can be produced with less working capital (α_{ic}), again via a higher α value. This is formalized in terms of Equations 3.2 and 3.3, where α, the productivity of working capital, is expressed as a function of e_{ic}, energy consumption, and o_{ic}, organization-related variables.

$$V_{ic} = \alpha[e_{ic}, o_{ic}]\omega_{ic} \qquad (3.2)$$

$$V_{ik} = \alpha[e_{ik}, o_{ik}]\omega_{ik} \qquad (3.3)$$

Consider the following case study, namely the manufacture of paper over time.

3.2.1 Case Study: The Manufacture of Paper

Like all production processes, paper making consists of transforming the state and shape of fibrous raw materials. In early times, paper was made from materials such as rags, hemp, and fish nets. Today, it is made, almost exclusively, from wood fibers. The process of paper making per se has, like all other processes, undergone important modifications over time. Pulping methods have been numerous, including soda pulp, sulfate pulp, sulfite pulp, mechanical pulp, semi-mechanical pulp, and thermomechanical pulp. Of more concern to us here, however, is the actual making of the paper.

From 200 BC to roughly the beginning of the 19th century, paper making (from pulp) was artisanal in nature. That is, paper was made by hand. In 1779, Nicolas-Louis Robert invented the first continuous paper machine. "It consisted of a vat in which an elongated paddle wheel lifted diluted pulp onto a continuous moving, endless, horizontal belt of wire mesh through which the water drained. Then the wire together with the drained web passed through a press similar to a clothes wringer" (Clark 1985, 1022). Improvements by Henry and Sealy Fourdrinier increased both the speed and performance of the early Robert continuous-flow paper machine. By 1827, the average paper machine had a wire 60 inches wide and operated at a speed of 25 feet per minute, producing 85 pounds of paper per hour. Today, modern Fourdrinier paper machines are over five times as wide, more than a hundred times as fast, and produce well over five hundred times as much paper as in 1827. Productivity increases, it therefore follows, have come about largely as the result of greater operating speeds. The latter were made possible by improvements in electric-drive technology, specifically, by the development of high-speed electric motors. For given paper machines, and given supervision (workers), output per paper machine (fixed wire size) has increased at unimaginable rates. For example, in January 1999, the Aylesford Newsprint Company in Kent, Great Britain, broke the speed record by 9.75 ft/min. The new record now stands at 5,261.75 ft/min.

Table 3.1 presents the technical specifications of a greenfield thermomechanical pulp (TMP)-based newsprint mill in the mid-1980's. The average daily capacity was 550 tons per day; the average speed of the machine was 3,750ft/min. Such a TMP mill required approximately 170 production workers (lower-level supervision), and 85 salaried workers (upper-level supervision). The capital costs are broken down into (1) machinery and equipment, (2) buildings, and (3) land.

Table 3.1
Thermomechanical Pulp-Based Newsprint Mill–Technical Specifications

Capacity	Annual	192,500 tons/year
	Daily	550 tons/day
Capital Costs	Machinery and Equipment	$125,000,000
	Buildings	$32,250,000
	Land	$5,000,000
	Total	$162,250,000
Labor	Production Workers	2 man hours/ton
	Salaried Workers	1 man hour /ton

Source: Anderson, Bonsor and Beaudreau (1982).

Table 3.2 presents what the industry refers to as "manufacturing costs" per finished ton, net of wood costs, but gross of transport. We see that per unit cost per finished ton is $102.00 which corresponds to $\alpha\omega_{ic}$ in Equation 2.1 in Chapter 2.

Table 3.2
Thermomechanical Pulp-Based Newsprint Mill–Manufacturing Costs Per Finished Ton

Labor Costs	$32.00
Maintenance and Operating Supplies	$24.00
Taxes and Insurance	$12.00
Transportation Costs	$34.00
Total	$102.00

Source: Anderson, Bonsor and Beaudreau (1982).

Let us now consider various "technological changes." First, suppose that, like the Aylesford Newsprint Company, the necessary changes are made to increase the machine speed 36 percent to 5,261.75 ft/min. In this case, the throughput rate increases as the result of a higher energy consumption rate (see Equation

3.1). Overall electric power consumption increases. Per unit electric power consumption will either increase, or, at the very best, remain constant. What is important to note here is the fact that such a change, while defined as "technological change" corresponds, in actual fact, to energy deepening, so to speak.[2] It is also important to note that the increase in output (value-added) is achieved with the same capital and labor (tools and supervision).

Cast in terms of Equation 3.2, such a change will be captured by an increase in α, the average and marginal productivity of operating capital (ω_{ic}). As such, for a given amount of labor, more output (work) will result. An important feature of speed up-based productivity increases is their ratchet-like nature. Speed-ups can, for a given level of supervision $S(t)$ and tools $T(t)$, increase the level of work per period of time $W(t)$; however, for a fixed level of work $W(t)$, they do not decrease the level of supervision $S(t)$ and tools $T(t)$. This owes mainly to the lumpiness of supervision and tools.

Second, consider supervision-related changes, specifically, the substitution of inanimate forms of supervision for animate supervision. Not long ago, the production of paper (newsprint and kraft) was animate supervision intensive. Product quality and machine performance were monitored by workers. Today, most of these functions are performed automatically by "control systems."

> The papermaking Group consumes pulp, water, steam and power and returns white water and condensate. The throughput of the paper grade has a set of specifications in terms of targets and limits for quality variables such as basis weight, moisture, caliper, ash, smoothness, formation, strength, optical properties and fault level. Many of these properties are measured on-line by either scanning or single-point sensors. Other attributes or properties, of the paper are either determined by human inspection or by laboratory testing. Automatic control of quality variables in both the machine direction (MD) and cross-direction (CD) is common practice, based on measurements from the on-machine sensors located immediately prior to the reel. Automatic control of the MD properties based on laboratory tests is practiced at some mills. (Brewster 1990, 45)

Let us suppose that further developments in sensor technology reduce even further the number of attributes and properties determined by human inspection. In this case, the number of workers—initially at 170—decreases say by half. As a result, with the newsprint machine producing at 5,261.75 ft/min, it stands to reasons that the cost per ton will decrease. Cast in terms of Equation 2.1, the remaining workers (animate supervisors) will be more productive, as indicated by a higher α value. That is, a given amount of value added (V_{ic}) will now require less working capital (ω_{ic}).

3.3 Energy Deepening-Based Rents

It has been argued that energy deepening, defined as an increase in energy use per capita, per period of time, ranks among the key factors in the rise of material civilization (Odum and Odum 1976; Rosenberg and Birdzell 1986; Beaudreau 1998,1999a). From Neolithic man's use of draft animals to till his fields, to the use by the ancient Egyptians of the thermal energy in the wind to propel their boats, to the use of water by Richard Arkwright to turn spindles, to the use of fossil fuels by British to weave cloth, the increased consumption of energy has led to an increase in the level of material wealth, not to mention the non-negligible improvement in the quality of life made possible by the substitution of inanimate forms of energy for muscular energy. Consequently, today, the contemporary worker, for the most part, no longer works; rather, s/he supervises (Beaudreau 1998).

This raises a number of interesting questions. For example, what led to this manifold increase in the level of per capita energy consumption? Why did Homo-sapiens-sapiens abandon muscle-based brawn, in favor of alternate forms of drive? What led British merchants to abandon the putting-out system (cottages) in favor of the gathering-in system (factories) to transform cotton, wool, linen, and other fibers? What led Henry Ford to electrify the assembly line, and, in the process, unleash the second industrial revolution? The answer, I submit, is what I refer to as energy rents, specifically financial (monetary) energy rents. Energy rents are defined as the difference between the value (utility or profits) of an incremental unit of energy, and its cost. For example, if the (expected) monetary gain from an additional *kWh* is greater than its cost, then the (expected) monetary energy rents are positive. In the cases described above, expected monetary energy rents were positive, prompting profit-maximizing producers to adopt more energy-intensive production processes. David Nye, in *Electrifying America*, pointed out that:

> Businessmen regarded electrification differently than did the general public, the intellectuals, or the emerging technical elite. As readers of Century, Success, Magazine of Wall Street, World's Work, and similar publications, they saw it not as a potentially dangerous form of social power, more as a utopian technology, nor as a mysterious new power in medicine, nor as a tool for rationalizing society. Rather, they embraced electrification as an instrument for

making profits. Led by the electrical industry, between 1890 and 1920, businessmen defined electricity as a commodity rather than a public service. Businessmen and investors knew early that electricity might be useful in almost any branch of commerce or industry. (Nye 1990, 168)

3.3.1 Utility-Based versus Monetary Energy Rents

Another way of seeing energy rents is in terms of arbitrage, specifically energy rent-based arbitrage. Clearly, if the expected returns from energy deepening are just equal to the expected costs, then there will be no incentives to increase energy intensity. This is also the case if the expected costs exceed the expected returns. It follows that only when rents can be earned (expected rents) will producers opt for more energy-intensive production techniques.

The same logic, one could argue, applies to all forms of energy deepening. Take, for example, the shift from draft animals (oxen and horses) to fossil fuel-powered internal-combustion engines as the source of motive drive. Whether it be for transportation or work, the move from one to the other was based on the presence of positive "energy rents."

As will be shown in this chapter, expected financial energy rents are the main underlying cause of underincome. Specifically, potential output increases more than actual output, potential income increases more than actual income, and potential expenditure increases more than actual expenditure, resulting in what I refer to as underincome.

3.4 From Animate to Inanimate Motive Power

Two events in 18th-century Great Britain changed the industrial landscape forever. The first was Richard Arwright's water-wheel-driven spinning jenny, while the second was the development and widespread diffusion of the Watts-Boulton rotative-power steam engine. Analytically-speaking, Arkwright's water-powered spinning jenny was of monumental importance, as it altered fundamentally the nature of work. The force required to spin cotton and wool would, from this point on, cease to be animate (muscle-based), but would be inanimate. Spinning wheels (spindles) would be powered by hydraulic power, transmitted by way of complex belting, gearing and shafting. This de facto lifted the energy constraint. Never again would human muscular power limit the amount of work done. According to Peter Stearns:

More impressive developments occurred in the preparatory phases in cotton, James Hargreaves invented a spinning jenny device about 1764, which mechanically drew out and twisted fibers into threads—though this advance too initially was applied to handwork, not a new power source. Carding and combing machines, to ready the fiber prior to spinning, were developed at about the same time. Then in 1769, Richard Arkwright developed the first water-powered spinning machine; it twisted and wound threads by means of flyers and bobbins operating continuously. These first machines were relevant only for the cheapest kind of thread, but other inventions by 1780 began to make possible the spinning of finer cotton yarns. These new devices also could be powered by steam engines as well as waterwheels. The basic principles of mechanized thread production have not changed to this day, though machines were to grow progressively larger, and a given worker could tend to a number of spindles. (Stearns 1993, 23)

Illustrating this is Matthew Boulton's Soho Factory in Bolton, which produced watch chains, platted wares and many other items using the hydraulic power of Hockley Brook as its principal drive source. Hockley Brook, however, posed a number of problems. For example, in the summer, water levels were, often times, insufficient to power the wheels, bringing the manufactory to a halt. To overcome this problem, Boulton turned to steam power, ordering a Savery engine to pump water and, in the process, turn the water wheels. According to Richard Hills:

In light of subsequent history, one of the most important people to consider using a Savery engine was Matthew Boulton when he wished to supplement the water resources of the Hockley Brook which powered his new Soho Manufactory. He had purposely moved out of Birmingham in 1765 to avoid operating an expensive horse mill, but the growth of the Manufactory presented him, with a similar dilemma once more. So his mind turned to employing a steam engine to lift water from the tail race of the waterwheel back to the mill dam. (Hills 1989, 40)

Realizing that steam could drive machinery directly—as opposed to via waterwheels—Boulton began work with James Watt in 1768 on what was to become the defining energy innovation of the 18th century, namely the Boulton-Watt rotary-drive steam engine. These developments, I argued in Beaudreau (1998), are essential to understanding Adam *Smith's An Inquiry into the Nature and Causes of the Wealth of Nations*. According to the record, Smith knew Boulton and Watt, and had personally visited the Soho Manufactory prior to 1776. *The*

Wealth of Nations, in essence, is an ode to the virtues of inanimate energy, fantastic, unimaginable wealth being the principal one.

The late 18th century/early 19th century, it therefore follows, was a transitional period, with animate, muscular energy being replaced by inanimate, hydraulic-based energy, which, in turn, was replaced by inanimate, fossil-fuel-based energy in the form of steam power. According to Katrina Honeyman:

> During the period 1780–1825, cotton factories varied not only in scale but also in type. S. D. Chapman has identified what he sees as three main types. The Type A mill was a small-scale operation, often employing hand-operated jennies or mules and possibly horse capstans for driving card machines. The cost of establishing and equipping this type of mill was about £1,000–£2,000. The Type B factory was more often purpose-built and comprised three or four storeys. It came in two sizes: one designed to hold approximately 1,000 spindles and requiring up to £3,000 investment; and one at least twice as large with up to 3,000 spindles, costing from £5,000. These are often referred to as Arkwright-type mills. Type C was larger, generally steam-powered, and cost about £10,000. This category of mill was not usual until the early 19th century. (Honeyman 1982, 57)

The substitution of inanimate power for animate, muscular power occurred over a period of roughly 100 years (1760–1860). Figure 3.1, based on data from B.R. *Mitchell's British Historical Statistics* on the numbers of workers employed in the U.K. cotton industry from 1806 to 1862, shows that by 1833, there were as many factory workers (lower-level supervisors) as hand weavers, and that by 1862, the latter had, for all intents and purposes, disappeared from the industry. Inanimate energy had completely displaced animate energy; animate supervision, however, remained.

Figure 3.1
Numbers Employed in the Cotton Industry 1806–1862

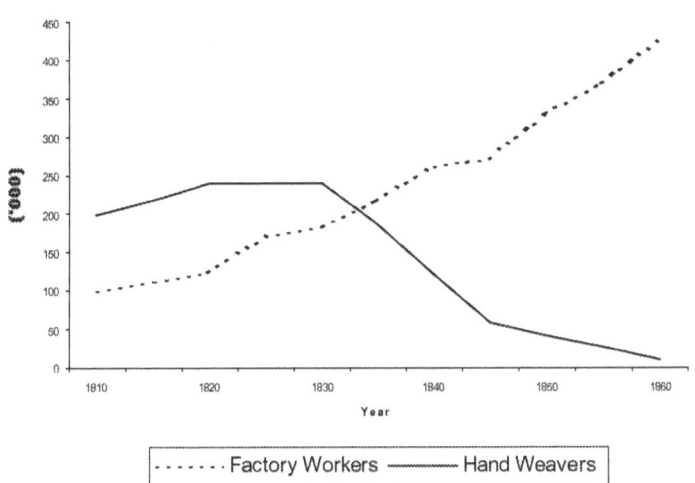

3.4.1 The Inanimate Power Revolution

The Importance of Speed

The manifold increase in U.K. manufacturing output in the 19th century resulted from, as argued here, the intensive energy-deepening which characterized much of this period. The energy deepening in question was achieved in two distinct ways, namely intensively and extensively. Starting with the latter, extensive energy deepening refers to the increase in the number and capacity of spindles and looms in the cotton industry. With Arkwright's spinning jenny, the number of spindles in the U.K. cotton spinning industry increased manifold. Similarly, with the advent of power looms, the weaving capacity, as measured by the size and number of looms, increased manifold.

Table 3.3
Coal and Cotton Consumption, Factory Workers, and Money Supply—
Levels and Growth Rates 1755–1860

Year	Coal	Growth	Cotton	Growth	Workers	Growth	Money	Growth
1755	4,230							
1760	4,520	0.06						
1765	4,950	0.09						
1770	5,520	0.11						
1775	6,120	0.10						
1780	6,750	0.10						
1785	7,555	0.11						
1790	8,570	0.13						
1795	9,570	0.11						
1800	10,960	0.14	52					
1805	12,960	0.18	59	0.13				
1810	14,790	0.14	124	1.10	100			
1815	16,590	0.12	81	-0.34	114	0.14		
1820	18,900	0.13	120	0.48	126	0.10		
1825	20,900	0.15	167	0.39	173	0.37		
1830	24,800	0.18	248	0.48	185	0.06		
1835	29,560	0.19	318	0.28	220	0.18	18,207	
1840	35,270	0.19	459	0.44	262	0.19	16,839	-0.08
1845	41,706	0.18	607	0.32	273	0.04	20,674	0.18
1850	50,968	0.22	588	-0.03	331	0.21	19,448	0.06
1855	64,500	0.26	839	0.42	371	0.12	19,830	0.02
1860	80,000	0.24	1,084	0.29	427	0.15	21,252	0.06

Source: Beaudreau (1999a).

A second source of energy deepening were the many speed-ups that character-ized the U.K. textiles industry in the 19th century. Existing machines, be they spin-ning or weaving, were speeded up, making for greater output per period of time. Characteristic of such "speed-ups" was an increase in power consumption per period in time, in keeping with the basic premises of energy-organization analysis. Improvements in steam engines throughout the 19th century, along with improve-ments in spinning and weaving *per se*, paved the way for increases in the throughput rates per unit of capital (i.e. spindle or loom). Among these was the development and commercial use of the high-pressure steam engine by Richard Trevithick and Arthur Woolf, which increased markedly the speed of execution, and consequently, the rate of output (throughput).

References to speed-ups in the early 19th century are few and far-between. However, the few that do exist convey the essence of the power revolution that was playing itself out in Great Britain. Take, for example, William Longston's testimony on the question of working conditions in the textiles industry before the Committee on the Factories Bill.

9397.   Is the intensity of application and of labour altered, either against or in favour of the operative and of the children employed in mills and factories?—I was a great number of years out of any factory, but those who were my acquaintances during my boy-hood have often conversed with me, and they very frequently say that it cannot be less than double in intensity and exertion of physical application.

9398.   State why you believe that the labour of those employed has doubled since the first introduction and use of cotton machinery, or at least since you first knew it?—The reason why I believe so is from some calculations which I have been obliged to make, and by my own observation during the time I was manager of a mill in 1830 and 1831, when I had some of the same operations under my own observation.

9399   Have you any objection to put in those calculations?—Certainly not. [The following document was then put in and read.]

9400.   It appears by this document that the work done is very greatly increased between the years 1810 and 1832; has the machinery been so altered as to produce that amazing difference, or does it result from accelerating the speed of the machin-ery?—It is from accelerating the speed generally; and another cause is, that more and more exertion is required from the individual working at the machine; these are the two causes.

9401.   Those two causes, then, prove what you have been asserting, namely that double the labour and attendance is now requisite that was formerly required?—I think so.

9402.   In spite of the improvements of machinery?—Yes; I believe those that are now work-ing in the same employment as I did when I was a boy, do double the work.

9403.   So that there may be a great improvement in machinery, and at the same time a great increase in actual labour to each operative?—Yes.

9404.   Has that been, as far as your experience has extended, the consonant result of improvements of machinery in those mills, namely, that the labour of the hands has increased with every improvement in the machinery; rather than diminished?—Yes; the improvements in the machinery have been great, and the same physical exer-tion, and the same physical exertion, and the same attention as was formerly applied, would certainly produce, in proportion to the altered state of machinery, a much greater quantity and better articles; but, added to that, the increased exertions make the quantities to be such as just now surprised you. (Committee on Factories Bill 1832, 430)

As is clear from his testimony, machinery speed-ups increased considerably the amount of "work" demanded of the corresponding "lower-level" supervisors.

This was the direct result of the fact that not all processes and sub-processes were automated. Faster-turning spindles and faster-operating looms required more exertion on the part of the "operatives"—that is, those who supervise the machinery (machine operatives). As the data presented show, output per lower-level supervisor (stretcher) increased by 200 percent from 1810 to 1832. In the case of mule yarn-spinning, the number of hanks spun, for 480 spindles (ceteris paribus), increased by 50 percent between 1806 and 1832.

3.4.2 The Role of Capital and Labor

The shift from the domestic system to the factory system altered the nature of both capital and labor. Labor, a source of energy (animate, muscular) and thus of motive drive in the domestic system, was reduced to a supervisory input, overseeing the workings of continuous-flow machinery. The men, women and children who, in the domestic system, had spun and woven cotton, wool, linen, etcetera, would, from now on, supervise the workings of steam-power driven spinning and weaving machines, and managing the various feed-stocks (inputs and outputs) in factories. Alfred Marshall described this far-reaching change in 1890 in the following terms:

> We may now pass to the effects which machinery has in relieving that excessive muscular strain which a few generations ago was the common lot of more than half the working men even in such a country as England…in other trades, machinery has lightened man's labours. The house carpenters, for instance, make things of the same kind as those used by our forefathers, with much less toil for themselves… Nothing could be more narrow or monotonous than the occupation of a weaver of plain stuffs in the old time. But now, one woman will manage four or more looms, each of which does many times as much work in the course of a day as the old hand loom did; and her work is much less monotonous and calls for much more judgment than his did. (Marshall 1890, 218)

The key word here is "manage." The woman he referred to now "manages," and, hence, no longer weaves. Moreover, as he pointed out, each power loom "does many times as much work in the course of a day as the old hand loom did." Conventionally-defined labor productivity, it follows, increased manifold.[3] E. Baines, in the *History of the Cotton Manufacture* published in 1835, refers to a tenfold increase in productivity for weavers.

A very good hand weaver, 25 or 30 years of age, will weave two pieces of 9-8ths shirting per week, each 24 yards long, containing 100 shoots of weft in an inch; the reed of the cloth being a 44 Bolton count, and the warp and weft hanks to 40 hanks to the lb. In 1823, a steam-loom weaver, about 15 years of age, attending two looms, could weave seven similar pieces in a week. In 1826, a steam-loom weaver, about 15 years of age, attending to two looms, could weave twelve similar pieces in a week; some could weave fifteen pieces. In 1833, a steam-loom weaver, from 15-20 years of age, assisted by a girl about 12 years of age, attending to four looms, can weave eighteen similar pieces in a week; some can weave twenty pieces. (Baines 1835, 240)

However, at this point in time, an important distinction is in order, namely, that between energy-based measures of productivity and organization-based measures of productivity. In the domestic system, workers physically exerted themselves, spinning and/or weaving, in addition to supervising the workings of their animate energy (i.e. their body) and the tools (rudimentary spinning wheels and hand looms). In the factory system, their responsibilities (job definition) were reduced considerably. Specifically, they would consist almost uniquely of supervision. As such, it follows that the relevant productivity measure as found in the factory system is organization-based (see Table 2.1).

Capital also underwent a major transformation. Specifically, the simple tools of the domestic system (spinning wheels and hand looms) were fitted with a power source (rotative power). Machinery, as a result, consisted of rudimentary tools fitted with an inanimate power source. Complex shafting, belting and gearing systems were used to transmit the torque generated by Watt-Boulton steam engines to the spindles and the looms. Capital costs per spindle or per square yard of weaving capacity increased substantially, owing to power-related costs, and to the need for more reliable spindles and looms.[4] Under the domestic system, spinning wheels and hand looms were fashioned out of wood (hardwood and softwood), harvested, in most cases, in local forests. The demands of high-throughput, continuous-flow production, however, were such that metal spindles and looms were needed, increasing, as such, the cost of capital. This, as it turns out, was true of all steam power-driven industries. These costs figured prominently in the works of classical political economists. The new drive technology required massive investments, both in steam engines, and in the accompanying tools. Saving and investment would, over the next half century, occupy center stage in political economy.

3.4.3 The Steam Engine and the Advent of Industrial Exchange Technology

The commercial application of the steam engine (the Watts-Boulton rotary steam engine) to drive spindles and looms in Great Britain did more than mark the beginning of a new, glorious era in the history of material civilization, it altered, in a non-negligible way, the exchange technology. Specifically, it transformed the producer into a market-coordinating agent, similar to the merchant. In cottage industries, the head of the family (extended family) coordinated the transformation of wool, cotton, and/or linen within the family. For example, in periods of heavy demand (for textiles), s/he could call upon a cousin, or sister-in-law to work the traditional hand- and foot-powered spinning machines and looms. Payment for services rendered would be made once the output in question was sold (delivered) to the merchant.

The move out of the "cottage" and into the "factory" changed all of this. Now, producers would have to coordinate their activities in a market setting, purchasing labor, energy (in this case, coal), and other factor inputs (excluding capital). As it turns out, this created a new demand for operating capital (i.e. ω). Producers now had to finance their variable costs using bank credit. In terms of the model presented in Chapter 2, this corresponds to the situation in which Equations 2.17 and 2.18 were added to Equation 2.9 to define the overall demand for operating capital. Clearly, the demand for operating capital increased by the amount of total variable costs.

These changes, however banal they may appear, mark the birth of the "industrial" exchange technology that is with us today. Today, as then, producers demand operating capital to finance their variable costs, while merchants demand operating capital to finance their activities (stocking/merchandising of consumption and capital goods). The overall demand for operating capital, per dollar value of value added, it therefore follows, is greater than one.

3.4.4 Cottages, Factories and The Problem of Underincome

Here, I examine the problem of underincome in the context of the industrial revolution. More specifically, in the context of the transition in Great Britain from cottage-based industry to factory-based textile industry. For purposes of exposition, it will be assumed that the transition in question occurred at a specific point in time, and, moreover, was complete. That is, at time T, the putting-out system was replaced instantaneously and completely by the gathering-in system.

Assuming that the demand for textile value added was, to begin with, equal to the supply of textile value added, it follows that the problem confronting U.K. textile producers, each having substantially more productive capacity, was one of markets. Would merchants' orders of textiles increase commensurately with productive capacity?

It follows from Chapter 2 that merchants will increase orders of textiles if and only if income (ω) rises, assuming that textiles are not an inferior good (suppose an income elasticity of unity). The relevant issue is the effect of the shift, at time T, to the factory system, on the overall level of money income (operating capital). Did the resulting level of operating capital (paid out to variable factor inputs) lead merchants to increase, in a commensurate fashion, their orders of textiles? If not, then inertia would set in. Producers would not increase output for lack of orders from merchants, and merchants would not increase orders for lack of operating capital (from producers). This describes what I refer to as "transitional" underincome. That is, the level of income, in this case, producer operating capital, does not increase commensurately with productive capacity, resulting in overcapacity, overproduction (perhaps), falling prices (perhaps), and overall inertia.[5]

Unfortunately, the evidence of underincome in the U.K. economy presented here is, for the most part, circumstantial, owing to data problems. Data on total productive capacity both before and after the shift out of cottages into factories, and on total operating capital (income) are not available (inexistent).

3.4.5 The Problem of Energy Deepening-Based Underincome

As A. E. Musson has argued, the power revolution in Great Britain in the 19th century, was not a one-shot event, consisting of the introduction of the Watts-Boulton rotary engine, but, instead, was a rather long and protracted affair, extending throughout much of the 19th century, and involving such subsequent innovations as the high-pressure, non-condensing steam engine (Woolf and Threvithick) and steam turbine technology (Parsons). Energy deepening, defined as the increase in energy use/consumption per period of time and per capita, occurred throughout the 19th century in Great Britain.

> It is generally recognized that the introduction of steam power was a crucial factor in the Industrial Revolution, closely linked with the exploitation of

Britain's coal and iron resources, the development of mechanical engineering, and the growth of the factory system. A considerable amount of historical research has been carried out into the scientific-technological developments involved—into how the steam engine was developed from the crude creations of Savery and Newcommen to the comparatively sophisticated products of Watt's genius, with separate condenser, air pump, direct action, rotative motion, etc.—and how steam power began to spread into coal-mining, cotton spinning, flour milling, brewing, and various other industries in the eighteenth century... In contrast to the interest in the early pioneering, there has been comparatively little effort to investigate the massive growth and spread of steam power after 1800, except in a few industries and areas. Several factors have contributed to this neglect. The "heroic" theory of historical evolution has tended to concentrate attention primarily on Newcommen and Watt, though with some interest in Trevithick and Woolf for their early development of high-pressure engines. (Musson 1976, 415)

With each increase in energy consumption per period of time came a proportional increase in the rated capacity of existing machinery. These are typically referred to as speed-ups. Consequently, existing machinery turned out more yarn or string, and, more cloth per period of time.

The problem, however, was finding an outlet for it. Did the demand for cloth and other manufactures increase commensurately? If so, then how? Referring to Equation 3.2, energy deepening will increase α, thus increasing the level of value added per dollar of operating capital. Merchants, however, have no private incentives to increase orders of textiles in the absence of an increase in operating capital (ω). The result: underincome and income inertia.

3.4.6 Evidence

The model predicts that, in the presence of energy deepening, productive capacity will increase more rapidly than the demand for and supply of operating capital, and consequently, the level of output, income and expenditure. To prove the existence of energy deepening-based underincome in 19th century Great Britain, one would require extensive time-series data on productive capacity growth and working capital (income) growth in the textile industry. Unfortunately, such data are not available. In light of this, various proxies were used.

Specifically, data on aggregate coal consumption and aggregate raw cotton consumption were used to proxy productive capacity growth, and data on money in circulation were used to proxy income (working capital) growth. For example, referring to Table 3.3, in the five-year interval 1850–1855, total coal consumption in the U.K. increased 26.5 percent, raw cotton consumption increased 42.6 percent, factory employment increased 12 percent, while money in circulation increased 1.9 percent. Admittedly, while these are imperfect proxies for capacity growth and income growth, they are nonetheless suggestive. Specifically, while Great Britain's ability to transform raw materials (add value) had increased substantially, its level of money income had not.

Table 3.4
Total Power Consumption, Textiles, Great Britain 1835–1903

Cotton

Year	Steam	Water	Total	Employment	$E_c(t)/S_c(t)$
1838	46	12	58	259	0.2239
1850	71	11	82	331	0.2477
1856	87	9	96	379	0.2532
1861	281	12	293	452	0.6482
1867	190	12	202	401	0.5037
1870	299	8	307	450	0.6822

Wool

Year	Steam	Water	Total	Employment	$E_c(t)/S_c(t)$
1838	17	10	27	87	0.3103
1850	23	10	33	154	0.2142
1856	31	9	40	167	0.2395
1861	53	11	60	173	0.3699
1867	85	12	97	262	0.3702
1870	103	12	115	239	0.4811

Miscellaneous

Year	Steam	Water	Total	Employment	$E_c(t)/S_c(t)$
1838	7	4	11	42	0.2619
1850	11	3	14	68	0.2058
1856	14	4	18	80	0.2250
1861	32	4	36	94	0.3829
1867	42	5	47	135	0.3489
1870	52	5	57	146	0.3904

Source: Mitchell (1988).

This finding, while consistent with the predictions of the theory, must be viewed as tentative at best. Remember, there is no direct evidence that money income in the textile industry did not increase in step with potential output. Let us now turn to other sources of evidence. As pointed out above, producers experiencing substantial increases in productive capacity can do either of three things. They can (1) produce at capacity, and literally flood the market with thread, yarn, or cloth, (2) continue producing at previous levels, maintaining price, or, (3) choose some combination thereof. The output data presented in Table 3.3, in combination with the price data presented in Columns 3 and 5 of Table 3.5, indicate that U.K. textile producers chose (1), namely to increase output, provoking price decreases throughout much of the 19th century.

Table 3.5
Price Indexes, United Kingdom 1805–1871

Year	Agriculture	Industry	Raw Cotton	Cotton
1805	175	166		
1810	190	198		
1815	164	164		
1819	110	134	9.58	11.73
1827	128	106	6.56	8.51
1835	118	106	10.25	6.53
1851	94	89	5.52	3.43
1861	117	114	8.56	3.38
1871	119	112	8.56	3.73

Table 3.5 presents price indexes for the period 1805 to 1871. We see, for example, that the price of raw cotton declined from 1819 to 1851, only to rise in the 1860's, the result of the U.S. Civil War which cut off cotton exports to the U.K. Column 5, which presents the price of cotton cloth, shows that it decreased monotonically from 1819 to 1871. One could argue that this reflected the general conditions of oversupply which characterized the industry for most of the 19th century. Cotton prices (price of value added) decreased monotonically.

Clearly, the U.K. market for textiles failed to grow commensurately with U.K. productive capacity, resulting in depressed prices. Adding to the woes of 19th century Great Britain were the nominal wage decreases that resulted. Theoretically speaking, lower prices need not necessarily result in lower wages (nominal), as productivity may have risen, which, of course, was the case here. Referring to Table 3.7, we see that wages "paid by a very respectable manufacturer (William Cannon) decreased monotonically from 1814 on, going from 20s,0d in 1814 to 3s,6d in 1833. Paradoxically, at a time in the history of material civilization when workers were the most productive (in the organizational sense), their wages and standard of living were decreasing monotonically.

3.4.7 Policy Responses

Understanding output, wage and price developments in the U.K. textile industry in the early 19th century, I maintain, is essential to understanding the ensuing policy debates, and, as will be shown later, the bulk of the writings in political economy in 19th century. In short, the development of the U.K. textile industry in the early 19th century stands as a microcosm of 19th- and 20th-century industrialization, namely more productive, but wallowing in depression. Here, I examine two 19th-century policy debates, namely, the creation of the *National Regeneration Society* in 1833, and the repeal of the Corn Laws in 1846. Both, I shall maintain, were responses to the problem of underincome, as described here. This will be followed by a look at what I refer to as "radical" policy debates, notably, Robert Owen's blueprint for a new form of social organization, namely the commune, and Karl Marx's blueprint for a new form of social organization, namely communism.[6] Both, I maintain, were responses to the problem of underincome, and its repercussions, both economic and social.

Table 3.6
Output and Input Prices, Selected U.K. Textiles 1815–1832

Second Quality 74s Calico Made by Power Loom

Year	Raw Material	Value Added	Product
1815	7s,0d	11s,0d	18s,0d
1824	3s,0d	6s,0d	9s,0d
1831	2s,0d	3s,9d	5s,9d
1832	2s,3.5d	3s,2.5d	5s,6d

Half-Elf Velveteens-20lbs. Weight

Year	Raw Material	Value Added	Product
1815	7s,0d	11s,0d	18s,0d
1824	3s,0d	6s,0d	9s,0d
1831	2s,0d	3s,9d	5s,9d
1832	2s,3.5d	3s,2.5d	5s,6d

30 Hanks Water Twist

Year	Raw Material	Value Added	Product
1815	7s,0d	11s,0d	18s,0d
1824	3s,0d	6s,0d	9s,0d
1831	2s,0d	3s,9d	5s,9d
1832	2s,3.5d	3s,2.5d	5s,6d

Source: Fielden (1833).

Table 3.7
Wages Paid by a Very Respectable Manufacturer (William Cannon)
1811–1833

Year	48 Reed	56Reed	70Reed
1811	10s,0d	13s,0d	20s,0d
1812	11s,1d	13s,6d	21s,0d
1813	13s,0d	16s,0d	22s,0d
1814	20s,0d	27s,0d	32s,0d
1815	11s,6d	15s,0d	21s,0d
1816	9s,0d	11s,0d	17s,0d
1817	6s,6d	8s,6d	13s,0d
1818	8s,0d	10s,0d	12s,6d
1819	7s,0d	9s,0d	11s,6d
1820	6s,6d	8s,0d	10s,6d
1821	8s,6d	10s,6d	12s,6d
1822	6s,0d	8s,6d	10s,6d
1823	6s,6d	8s,6d	10s,0d
1824	6s,6d	8s,6d	10s,0d
1825	6s,6d	8s,0d	10s,0d
1826	5s,0d	6s,6d	8s,6d
1827	4s,6d	5s,6d	8s,0d
1828	4s,6d	5s,6d	8s,0d
1829	4s,0d	5s,6d	8s,0d
1830	3s,6d	5s,0d	7s,0d
1831	3s,6d	5s,0d	7s,0d
1832	3s,6d	5s,0d	7s,0d
1833	3s,6d	5s,0d	7s,0d

Source: Fielden (1833).

By the 1830's, steam ("fire power") had conferred upon the U.K., especially its textile and iron industries, productive powers that far exceeded its income (aggregate working capital), resulting in generalized (within manufacturing) excess supply and price and wage deflation. As nominal product prices and wages fell, so did the "standard of living" in manufacturing, owing, in large measure, to the sectorial nature of the price deflation in question. Food prices, for example, remained relatively constant throughout the 19th century, despite the repeal of the Corn Laws in 1846. The ultimate irony had befallen the textile industry. More productive than ever before, working conditions and profit rates had deteriorated significantly. This provoked a number of policy debates, ranging from reforming the institution of profit maximization to free trade. For example, one finds the *National Regeneration Society*, advocating a coordinated reduction in output. The Society's ultimate goal, as outlined by John Fielden, was to improve the "condition of the productive classes."

> The proposal submitted to the productive classes, recommending them to lessen their productions, in some articles one-third, in order that they may improve their condition, is so novel and unprecedented in its character, and at first appears so much opposed to accomplish its end, that I should have felt some astonishment if it had not called forth the opposition of thinking men, who are not in possession of the facts which demonstrate the necessity there is for the productive classes to adopt such a course; so far, therefore, from felling any uneasiness at your conduct in condemning the proposal plan of eight hours' work for the present day's full day wages. (Fielden 1833, 10)

To this end, competition would have to give way to cooperation. Manufacturers would have to, as a group, reduce output, in the name of the public good. Unprecedented productivity growth in the textiles industry in the presence of excessive competition, Fielden argued, had contributed to lower wages and prices.

> These tables present a history of the works of those engaged in the cotton trade, for the eighteen years ending in 1832; and I have no hesitation in saying that history presents no parallel to a like increase in the taking away from the producers, for the those who do not produce... When nearly three times the quantity manufactured in 1832, was paid for with less money by two millions three quarters at thirteen millions, than little more than one third of the quantity commanded in 1815, and to manufacture which increased in 1832, more than double the number of persons were employed, can you wonder, sir, at the strange anomaly of increased production being accompanied by increased

and increasing distress among the manufacturers and their workmen? (Fielden 1833, 11)

Analytically, the *National Regeneration Society* advocated replacing unbridled competition, the effects of which were ubiquitous, with a form of industry-wide and economy-wide cooperation. Textile producers would agree to reduce output by ten percent, and work hours to eight. The problem, in other words, was, paradoxically, too much output, coupled with too much competition. By reducing output, nominal product prices would rise, restoring profit margins, and, in the process, increasing overall sector (labor and capital) welfare.

The second policy measure was the movement, initiated by Manchester producers and merchants, to repeal the Corn Laws, which imposed duties on imported "corn," or cereals. Manufacturers felt that by repealing the Corn Laws, U.K. imports of food would rise, thus lowering their price, and, more importantly, exports of textiles and other manufactures would rise, in keeping with "quid pro quo." Free trade would, as such, be a win-win strategy. First, lower cereal prices would, as David Ricardo argued, lower the cost of living, and, consequently, the cost of labor. Second, and more importantly (in 1846), it would stimulate foreign demand for U.K. finished goods, thus weakening the link between domestic wage income (aggregate working capital) and the demand for textiles on the part of U.K. merchants. Theoretically, it would solve the indeterminacy referred to earlier. Sales abroad would prompt merchants, independent of domestic wage income, to increase orders, thus stimulating the manufacturing sector.

As it turned out, this measure was preferred to the *National Regeneration Society's* call for industry-wide and economy-wide cooperation. The reasons were many. First, as pointed out, foreign trade alters the nature of the "exchange technology," weakening the role of domestic wage income in merchants' demand for textiles. Aggregate demand would, from then on, no longer depend solely on wage income in the U.K.[7]

Outlets would be found for U.K. textiles, thus arresting the price deflation. Also, "corn" could be imported at lower prices, eliminating any upward pressure on wages. A related policy development, I argue, was the *Bank Charter Act of 1843*, which imposed strict limits on the creation of trade credit by the private banks. Throughout this period, proponents of the Banking School maintained that the commercial crises were the direct result of overzealous banks, extending trade credit unscrupulously. Falling wages and prices were the result of an over-extended money supply (total trade credit). In order to prevent such occurrences, strict limits on credit would be required.

Ironically, the problem, as it turns out, was the lack of credit in the form of income (i.e. underincome). Producers had increased output without increasing, commensurately, money income, resulting in underincome. Not surprisingly, the *Bank Charter Act of 1843* failed to rid the U.K. of commercial crises. In fact, if anything, by restricting credit in a period of energy deepening, it may have, at least theoretically, provoked—or worsened—downturns. A more appropriate policy rule would have the level of outstanding trade credit increasing with potential output, the latter being highly correlated with overall power consumption.

3.4.8 Underincome and 19th-Century Political Economy

As has been shown here, the problem of underincome exacted a heavy toll on 19th century Great Britain. The general optimism of the early nineteenth century had turned to pessimism—not to mention, revolt—by mid-century. Nominal and real wages had fallen, bringing with them the standard of living, and the social fabric. Recessions became commonplace.

This raises a number of questions, notably, were 19th-century political economists aware of the problem of underincome? After all, political economy, as argued by Berg (1980), was an outgrowth of the "machine age."

> The machine was not an impersonal achievement to those living through the Industrial Revolution; it was an issue. The machinery question in early nineteenth-century Britain was the question of the sources of technical progress and the impact of the introduction of the new technology of the period on the total economy and society. The question was central to everyday relations between master and workman, but it was also of major theoretical and ideological interest. The very technology at the basis of economy and society was a platform of challenge and struggle.
>
> The machinery question was, furthermore, an issue which stimulated analysis in political economy during the key years of the formation of this new theoretical discipline. Political economists took up the theoretical debate on the introduction, diffusion, and social impact of the radically new techniques of production associated with the era. Recognizing that the machine formed the basis for an unprecedented economic transformation, political economists created new concepts and made growth potential and technological advances of the British economy the new focus of their analysis. (Berg 1980, 8)

What, according to them, was the cause of the problem? What was the solution? Unfortunately, the answer to the first question is no. Nineteenth-century political economists were, in general, unaware of the problem of underincome. While a number of writers, including Jean-Charles Léonard Sismonde de Sismondi and Thomas Malthus, raised the issue, no one fully understood it (Beaudreau 1999a).

Among the reasons for this, I maintain, was the state of exchange/monetary theory in the late 18th–early 19th centuries. As shown in Chapter 2, understanding the problem of underincome requires an understanding of the producer-merchant exchange technology that emerged in late 18th–early 19th century Great Britain. It therefore follows that to understand the intricacies of underincome, one had to first understand exchange. Unfortunately, political economy in the 19th century was not particularly deft in its study of, and, hence, understanding of monetary exchange. While writers like Adam Smith, described—sometimes at length—the financing of trade, no one provided an integral account of exchange similar to that presented in Chapter 2. In fact, from very early on (early 19th century), the bulk of macroeconomics was devoid of money and money income, focusing instead on real analysis. Such was the case in the debate opposing underconsumptionists and classical economists. Consider, to begin with, Smith's account of the nature of profits.

> First, it may be employed in raising, manufacturing, or purchasing goods, and selling them again with a profit. The capital employed in this manner yields no revenue or profit to its employer, while it remains in his possession, or continues in the same shape. The goods of the merchant yield him no revenue or profit till he sells them for money and the money yields him as little until it is again exchanged for goods. His capital is continually going from him in one shape, and returning to him in another, and it is only by means of such circulation, or successive exchanges, that it can yield him any profit. Such capitals, therefore, may very well be called circulating capitals. (Smith 1776, 133)

To Smith, profits are clearly a residual form of income. This, however, is of no apparent consequence. The problem of underincome is not broached, at least not directly. It is implicitly assumed that the value of circulating capital is identically equal to the value of production.

The problem of underincome, however, appears, albeit indirectly, in *The Wealth of Nations*. In Chapter III of Book I, entitled "That the Division of Labour is limited by the Extent of the Market," Smith argues that the division of labor—read, mechanization—is limited by the extent of the market.

> As it is the power of exchanging that gives occasion to the division of labour, so the extent of this must always be limited by the extent of that power, or, in other words, by the extent of the market. When the market is very small, no person can have any encouragement to dedicate himself entirely to one employment, for want of the power to exchange all that surplus part of his own labour, which is over and above his own consumption, for such parts of the produce of other men's labour as he has occasion for. (Smith 1776,136)

Clearly, this is a form of underincome, albeit an indirect one. According to Smith, the extent of the market determines the overall level of demand. What is important to note, however, is that, according to Smith, the market is a function of population, and population alone. Markets grow in size with the population. The division of labor, it therefore follows, is determined by population growth. The decision to mechanize production processes is, as such, tied to market size, which, in turn, is tied to population. Per-capita income growth (via increased wages or profits), as a determinant of the extent of the market, is ignored. Implicit is the problem of underincome referred to above, and, ironically, a refutation of Say's law, as demand creates supply, and not supply creating demand, as Smith's acolytes would go on to argue. Producer behavior in labor and capital markets have no bearing on the "extent of the market." Producers don't create markets; rather, population growth makes markets.

This having been said, there is evidence which suggests that some 19th- century writers were, at the very least, cognizant of exchange-related problems. One of these is Swiss political economist, Jean-Charles Léonard Sismonde de Sismondi, who spent considerable time in Great Britain in the early nineteenth century studying the process of industrialization. In *Principes d'économie politique*, published in 1819, he alluded to the problem of underincome, and, more importantly, noted its game-theoretical (strategic) aspects, specifically, the absence of private incentives to increase money income in response to a process-based technology shock.

> Le vendeur n'a pas par lui-même aucun moyen d'étendre son débit, qui ne réagisse sur ses confrères; il leur dispute une quantité donnée de revenu qui doit remplacer son capital; et plus, il réussit à en garder pour lui même; moins il en laisse pour les autres. Il ne dépend nullement du producteur d'augmenter les revenus de la société, ou du marché qu'il sert de manière qu'ils puissent s'échanger contre une augmentation de produits... Entre commerçants, on regarde comme une mauvaise action de se séduire réciproquement ses pratiques; mais la concurrence que chacun exerce contre tous ne présente point une idée aussi précise; et un commerçant n'a pas moins d'empressement

d'étendre son débit aux dépens de ses confrères qu'à le proportionner à l'accroissement des richesses, lorsque celles-ci lui offrent à l'échange d'un nouveau revenu. Jusqu'ici dans l'un ou l'autre cas, la découverte d'un procédé nouveau a causé une grande perte nationale, une grande diminution de revenu, et par conséquent, la consommation. (Sismonde de Sismondi 1819, 345)

Thomas Malthus, in *Principles of Political Economy Considered with a View to their Practical Applications*, pointed, although indirectly, to the problem of underincome, defining it as a "problem of distribution," distribution referring to the creation of income, and not the functional distribution of income.

> We have seen that the powers of production, to whatever extent they may exist, are not alone sufficient to secure the creation of a proportionate degree of wealth. Something else seems necessary in order to call these powers fully in action. This is effectual and unchecked demand for all that is produced. And what appears to contribute most to the attainment of this object, is, such a distribution of produce, and such an adaptation of this produce to the wants of those who are to consume it, as constantly to increase the exchangeable value of the whole mass…In the same manner, the greatest stimulus to the continued production of commodities, taken altogether, is an increase in the exchangeable value of the whole mass, before a greater value of capital has been employed upon them. (Malthus 1827, 361)

As these excerpts demonstrate, both Sismonde de Sismondi and Malthus were aware of the problem of underincome. The problem, according to them, was not with "creating" wealth, but rather in "distributing" it. Producers had no private incentives to increase wages, which, given the residual nature of profits, resulted in underincome.

It is my contention that the main obstacle to a more thorough understanding of the problem of underincome in the 19th century was the absence of an empirically-consistent model of exchange, akin to the producer-merchant model of exchange developed above. Underincome is, as I have demonstrated, an exchange-related problem. Yet, exchange issues were, for the most part, not even broached in the 19th century.

Another example of this is the debate surrounding what has since become known as Say's Law, attributed to nineteenth-century French political economist, Jean-Baptiste Say. According to William Thweatt, Say's law can be described in terms of a series of propositions:

1.   The production process (supply) generates the income necessary for the demand for these products, Money, therefore, is only an intermediary,

facilitating exchange and making it more efficient. Otherwise, in terms of the production process, it is only a veil when it comes to understanding the real economy.

2.   There is no need to worry about the possibility that some of the income generated in the production process will not be spent during exchange, at least not until that far-off day when everyone has had all his wants satisfied. In the more ordinary circumstances of the present world there is no likelihood of a leakage from the income-expenditure stream.

3.   Of course, partial overproduction of specific commodities by individual producers is possible if and when "mistakes" are made in the sense that commodities are produced in amounts not wanted at prices covering cost.

4.   As a consequence of (1) through (3), an economy cannot save too much, in the sense of accumulating capital goods too fast, so that it is not possible for it to have an excess of commodities or of a stock of capital. (Thweatt 1979, 81)

The issues raised by Sismonde de Sismondi and Malthus, as I have shown here, were related to exchange, and the exchange process. Paradoxically, Say's retort was devoid of exchange-related issues, to the point that Say cast most of his analysis in real terms. Clearly, the lack of an empirically-consistent model of exchange obfuscated—to the point of extinguishing—any potentially fruitful debate between Sismonde de Sismondi and Malthus on the one hand, and Say and Ricardo on the other hand.

This raises the question why? Why was 19th-century political economy devoid of empirically-consistent models of exchange? The answer, I submit, can be found in the dialectic that characterized the emerging field of political economy. As pointed out earlier, classical political economy was dialectic in nature, being the antithesis to mercantilism. As is well known, mercantilists equated money with wealth, with causality running from the former to the latter. Classical political economists, like their counterparts in moral philosophy, begged to disagree, arguing that the individual, more specifically, the free individual (vis-à-vis government), was the ultimate source of wealth.

All things mercantile were, as such, expunged from the public debate, with the result that exchange technologies were ignored. Political economy was cast in real terms, money being a veil, having no bearing whatsoever on real magnitudes. Problems ignored, however, are not problems solved. As we shall see next, the failure of 19th century political economists to provide an empirically-consistent model of exchange would come back to haunt the profession in the 20th century, which, like the 19th century, was hit by another massive, energy-based technology shock, namely electric power.

3.5 From Belts and Shafts to Electrons: Early 20th-Century Energy Deepening

The shift from the domestic to the factory system in the 19th century lifted and pushed back the energy constraint which had, for over two million years, constrained Homo sapien's (neanderthalensis and sapiens) ability to transform the earth's abundant supply of raw materials into goods and services. The energy constraint, however, had not been lifted completely, owing to (1) the limited applications of steam power, and (2) the associated power transmission technology, namely gearing, shafting and belting. Not all 19th-century production processes were amenable to steam power-based drive (i.e. driven by steam power). Steam engines were generally large (over 20h.p.), making them uneconomical for small-scale processes. Second, there was the problem of speed-ups. The belting, shafting and gearing transmission technology common to steam engines (Watt-Boulton) *de facto* limited speed ups, putting an upper bound on energy deepening.

> A factory's from of power determines its maximum size and possible locations. For 250 years water wheels supplied the majority of all industrial energy in the United States. Water power tied production to the banks of swiftly moving streams and required the construction of dams, channels, and spillways… Within the mill, energy had to be transmitted by gears, belts and pulleys, which lost power at literally every turn. In an economy based on such power transmission, the factory reached an absolute limit on its size beyond which inefficiencies were too great… Only in 1870 did steam engines supplant water power as the chief energy source, not so much through a process of replacement of existing facilities as in new plant construction, particularly in the Middle West where the flat terrain made water power less feasible than in the East or Far West. Steam-driven mills could be built away from streams, but they still had systems of gearing and belting. (Nye 1990, 194)

Enter a new power transmission technology, namely, electro-magnetic motors (hereafter, electric motors). Unlike steam engines, electric motors came in different sizes and more importantly, different—read, faster—speeds. As they began appearing in factories (in replacement of steam engines), the energy constraint was, once again, lifted and pushed back, in this case, further than any ever before. Production processes that had, hitherto, not been mechanized were. Henry Ford's electric motor-driven assembly line is a case in point.

Static material-handling processes, of which the final assembly of the automobile is a case in point, (i.e. the craft system) were replaced with continuous-flow materials handling processes, driven by direct-current [DC] electric motors. Secondly, production processes that were already mechanized (i.e. powered by steam) were converted to electric power, resulting in even greater speeds (throughput rates), and consequently, higher throughput and productivity. The result: the second industrial revolution. Electric power transformed industry, increasing throughput rates of existing mechanized processes, and mechanizing processes which had, until then, resisted inanimate power. Hand-held, electric power tools are a case in point. Electric drills, saws, and planners replaced hand drills, saws and planners.

This section proceeds in the same way as the previous section. I begin by examining the impact of electric power on U.S. industry, paying particular attention to the manufacturing sector. This is followed by a look at the policy responses, which, in turn, is followed by a look at its impact on 20th century political economy.

More versatile than belting, gearing and shafting, electric drive de facto removed the energy constraint, setting the stage for what turned out to be 75 years of energy deepening. Few were the sectors of the U.S. economy not affected by the new power transmission technology. Production processes driven by belting, gearing and shafting transmitting steam and hydraulic power were converted to electric drive, resulting in higher throughput rates. Those that had resisted "mechanization" were mechanized. Among these one finds the mining sector, the petrochemical sector, and the material handling sector in general. Electric motor-powered conveyor belts and pumps increased throughput rates in all of these sectors, resulting in substantially greater productivity. Analytically speaking, the introduction of electric drive ought be viewed as an extension of the first industrial revolution where, as argued earlier, inanimate power replaced animate, muscular power. The only difference was that now, the chemical energy found in fossil fuels would drive electro-magnetic generators, the output of which would, in turn, drive production processes.

According to Warren D. Devine Jr, the shift from shafting, belting and gearing drive to electric drive stands as one of the most rapid and complete transitions in "energy use" in recorded history.

Perhaps the most rapid and complete transition in energy use was the shift from steam power to electric power for driving machinery. Steam power prevailed at the turn of the century, with steam engines providing around 80 percent of the total capacity for driving machinery. By 1920, electricity had replaced steam as the major source of motive power, and by 1929—just forty-five years after their first use in a factory—electric motors provided 78 percent of all mechanical drive. (Devine 1990, 21)

Ignored by the economics profession, this change galvanized the engineering profession. Process and power engineers could hardly contain their enthusiasm. Consider, for example, the following quote taken from a speech by Matthew S. Sloan, President of the *New York Edison Company*, to the annual dinner of trust companies in Chicago in February 1929:

> Mr. Sloan compared this age which he termed the "new industrial revolution" with "the industrial revolution" in the eighteenth century, when the steamboat and locomotive came into use. As steam brought in the machine era, electricity, he said, has brought in the era of mass production which has so greatly affected the general economic situation and social conditions. Thus, electricity, he said, is responsible for our present production. With all its attendant circumstances of lowered unit costs, lowered prices, increased wages, intensifying merchandizing, wider markets, higher standard of living. Electricity-motivating machinery has multiplied the working power of the nation many times, he said, and the generating stations of the country now have a capacity of 35,000,000 horsepower, of the ability to do the work of about 350,000,000 men. In 1900, the generating capacity was only 3,000,000 horsepower. (New York Times, February 15, 1929)

In the same year, the *President's Conference on Unemployment*, chaired by Herbert C. Hoover, identified the electrification of U.S. industry as the "single most important change in U.S. industry." In its report, it described this far-reaching change as follows:

> Characteristic also has been the rise in the use of power—three and three-quarters times faster than the growth of population—and the extent to which power has been made readily available not alone for driving tools of increased size and capacity, but for a convenient purposes in the smallest business enterprise and on the farm and in the home. Factories no longer need to cluster about the source of power. Widespread interconnection between power plants, arising out of an increasing appreciation of the value of flexibility in power and made possible by technical advances during recent years, has created huge reservoirs of power so that abnormal conditions in one locality need

not stop the wheels of industry. The increasing flexibility with which electricity can be delivered from power has enabled manufacturers and farmers to meet high labor costs by the application of power-driven specialized machines; and, power in this flexible form has penetrated into every section of the United States, including many rural areas. The survey shows that as a nation we use as much electricity as all of the rest of the world combined. Through the subdivision of power, the unskilled worker has become a skilled operator, multiplying his effectiveness with specialized automatic machinery and processes. (National Bureau of Economic Research 1929, *xi*)

The shift to electric drive is easily formalized in terms of the energy-organization framework. Specifically, electric drive, by lifting the constraints imposed by belting, shafting and gearing transmission technology, allowed for greater inanimate energy consumption per period of time (i.e. $E(t)$). Higher energy consumption per unit time period increased throughput rates (output per period time) throughout U.S. industry, and for that matter, throughout the world, increasing conventionally-measured productivity. Output per lower-level supervisor (i.e. conventionally-defined labor productivity) increased substantially. In sectors where water, wind, or steam power had failed to penetrate, electric drive provided a flexible, made-to-scale, source of power, increasing productivity. As pointed out earlier, and highlighted in these quotes, there was hardly a sector of the U.S. economy that had not been affected in one way or another by electric drive.

Consider, for example, the mining sector, which had, throughout the 19th century, resisted "mechanization." Historian David E. Nye describes the application of electricity in the mining sector as follows:

Mine owners had many uses for electricity. Electric lights gave safe illumination that did not exhaust scarce oxygen supplies. Electric-alarm systems signaled danger or disaster. Electric drills were more portable than other drills: "Where electric power is used, small wires take the place of cumbersome pipes necessary for the transmission of steam or compressed air." Portable electric pumps often replaced steam engines, to keep pits free from water. An electric hoist had similar advantages over a steam-driven hoist; it was "more easily installed, and when in place takes up much less room than a steam outfit of the same hoisting capacity. It does away with the boiler, coal bins, and piping."... The greatest single change electricity made in the mines was the elimination of the mules, which were replaced by squat, powerful electric locomotives. With such equipment one company in Pennsylvania produced 11,000 tones of coal a month in the 1890's without using a single mule. With similar equipment New York and Scranton Coal company saved five or six cents per ton of coal extracted and the Hillside Coal and Iron Company saved almost $20,000 per year on the cost of mules and laborers."… At Green Ridge Colliery, for example, a station engineer, a motorman, and helper could run an electric locomotive that replaced six mule drivers, four boy helpers, and seventeen mules. (Nye 1990, 205)

How did the resulting energy deepening affect conventionally-defined productivity in U.S. manufacturing? That is, how did it affect α, the marginal revenue product of working capital (Equations 3.1 and 3.2)? As it turns out, this is a difficult issue to address, given the paucity of good time-series data. The data on productivity for this period are sparse and incomplete. Nonetheless, I proceeded to garner information on two fronts. First, I considered the case of the Ford Motor Company which, in 1913, moved from static assembly to electric power-driven dynamic assembly, commonly known as mass production. Second, a number of energy-based productivity measures were estimated for this period.

The choice of the Ford Motor Company (FMC) as a case study was based on its pioneering use of electric drive (Nye 1990; Beaudreau 1996a). It is worthwhile to note that its founder, Henry Ford, had been chief mechanical engineer at the Detroit Edison Illuminating Company from 1886 to 1899, a period of 14 years. In earlier work (Beaudreau 1996a), I argued that this period in Ford's life is essential to understanding of the development of high-throughput continuous-flow manufacturing at the FMC and, ultimately, in the United States, not to mention throughout the world. From then on, Ford was, to put it mildly, a power zealot, as evidenced by his life long friendship with Thomas Edison, and his attempt at securing the rights to the Muscle Shoals hydroelectric project in 1919. His single most important contribution to production technology, I argued in Beaudreau (1996a), was the application of electric drive to production and assembly processes, resulting in record increases in productivity (Nye 1990; Beaudreau 1996a).

Table 3.8
The Ford Motor Company, Assembly Process Productivity

Process	Phase	Assembly Time	Index
Magneto	Initial	20m,0s	100
	I	13m,10s	66
	II	7m,0s	35
	III	5m,0s	25
Transmission Cover	Initial	18m	100
	I	9m,0s	50
Chassis Assembly	Initial	12h,28s	100
	I	6h,0m	48
	II	1h,33m	12

Source: Beaudreau (1996a), 6.

To see this, consider Table 3.8, taken from Beaudreau (1996a), which presents throughput data measured per period of time. Prior to the introduction of electric drive-powered assembly lines, it took, on average, 20 minutes to assemble a magneto. In the initial phase of electric drive-powered assembly lines (i.e. conveyor belts), this was reduced to 13 minutes, followed by a further reduction to 7 minutes, and ultimately, to 5 minutes. Productivity, it therefore follows, had quadrupled. Even greater productivity gains were achieved in chassis assembly where the required time went from 12 hours, 28 minutes, to 6 hours, and eventually, to 1 hour, 33 minutes.

Figure 3.2
Ford Motor Company Productivity

Figure 3.2 presents standard labor productivity data, defined as the number of Model T's per worker. From a level of 8.36 in 1912, it climbed, mercurially, to 20.89 in 1915, a 150 percent increase. Electric drive had more than doubled productivity. In the 1926 edition of the *Encyclopedia Britannica*, Ford described "mass production" in the following terms:

> Mass production is not merely quantity production, for this may be had with none of the requisites of mass production. Nor is it merely machine production, which also may exist without any resemblance to mass production. Mass production is the focusing upon a manufacturing project of the principles of power, accuracy, economy, system, continuity, and speed. (Ford 1926, 821)

The operant words here are power and speed. Mass production, à la Ford, was about speed.[8] In little time, electric drive as applied at the Ford Motor Company spread throughout U.S., and, for that matter, throughout the world. According to historian David S. Hounshell:

> The story of mass production at the Ford Motor Company was not something only historians of a later generation would delve into and try to understand. Henry Ford's contemporaries, many of whom were competitors, closely

watched the doings at Highland Park, attempting to understand and emulate the revolutionary developments. Henry Ford encouraged their interest. Unlike the Singer Manufacturing Company, the Ford Company was completely open about its organizational structure, its sales, and its production methods... As a consequence of Ford's openness, Ford production technology diffused rapidly throughout American manufacturing. (Hounshell 1984, 260)

Consumption of electric power in U.S. manufacturing increased dramatically in the ensuing years. Referring to Table 3.10, we see that from a level of 9,250 million kilowatt hours in 1912, it had more than doubled by 1917 (i.e. 20,750 million kilowatt hours), and, doubled again by 1927. Cast in per-worker terms, in 1912, each manufacturing employee supervised 1,111 kilowatt hours of electric power. This doubled by 1917, tripled by 1923, and quadrupled by 1926.[9] Conventionally-defined productivity increased in step. Productivity indexes [V_{ic}/ω_{ic}] for this period show a marked increase. For example, the NBER productivity index goes from a level of 29.2 in 1912 to a level of 46.5 in 1926, a 60 percent increase.

Table 3.9
The Ford Motor Company, Production Data 1909–1916

Year	Employees	Model T's	Output Per Employee
1909	1,655	13,843	8.36
1910	2,773	20,727	7.47
1911	3,976	53,488	13.45
1912	6,867	82,388	11.99
1913	14,366	189,088	13.16
1914	12,880	230,788	17.91
1915	18,892	394,788	20.89
1916	132,702	585,388	17.90

Source: Beaudreau (1996a),152.

Like steam power a century and a half earlier, the shift to electric drive increased throughput rates, and, consequently, conventionally-defined labor productivity. It is important to point out, however, that conventionally-defined labor was not more productive; rather, employees were being called upon to supervise (oversee) the increased work done, in this case, by inanimate energy.

The second industrial revolution was, as such, a continuation of the first industrial revolution. Like the first, the key ingredient was power.

Table 3.10
U.S. Manufacturing Data 1912–1945

Year	Electric Power Consumption	Employees	Ratio	Productivity NBER
1912	9,250	8,322	1,111	29.2
1917	20,750	9,872	2,101	31.7
1920	26,913	10,702	2,514	32.0
1921	23,924	8,262	2,904	36.8
1922	27,364	9,129	2,997	41.8
1923	32,585	10,317	3,158	40.2
1924	34,967	9,675	3,614	42.8
1925	39,725	9,942	3,995	45.6
1926	46,350	10,156	4,563	46.5
1927	51,012	9,996	5,103	47.6
1928	52,699	9,942	5,300	49.7
1929	55,122	10,702	5,150	52.0
1930	53,930	9,562	5,640	52.3
1931	50,410	8,170	6,170	54.0
1932	43,504	6,931	6,276	50.5
1933	46,561	7,397	6,294	54.9
1934	50,593	8,501	5,951	57.4
1935	56,706	9,069	6,252	61.2
1936	62,949	9,827	6,405	61.6
1937	64,757	10,794	5,999	60.7
1938	58,452	9,440	6,191	59.9
1939	70,518	10,278	6,861	65.4
1940	83,276	10,985	7,580	68.7
1941	104,037	13,192	7,886	71.2
1942	122,762	15,280	8,034	72.4
1943	143,995	17,602	8,180	73.4
1944	145,015	17,328	8,368	72.5
1945	134,955	15,524	8,693	71.5

Source: Beaudreau (1996a).

3.5.1 Electric Power-Generated Underincome: The Evidence

To what extent had productivity growth outstripped wage—and consequently, income—growth in U.S. manufacturing? In this section, I examine the evidence.

Data on labor productivity, wages, and prices in U.S. manufacturing for the period 1920–1929 are used. Referring to Table 3.10, we see that manufacturing productivity as measured by the National Bureau of Economic Research's output per man-hour series increased 62 percent over the period in question, rising from 32 in 1920 to 52 in 1929. In spite of this, the nominal wage remained constant. In 1920, it stood at $0.55, while in 1929, it stood at $0.56. The real manufacturing wage, defined as the nominal wage divided by the consumer price level (1958=100), increased 31 percent over this period. What is important to note, however, is the fact that the major part of this increase came as the result of the Depression of 1921, when the price level fell from 65.4 to 50.1. Thus, the data are unequivocal: despite important productivity gains, producers in general resisted wage increases and price decreases. From 1922 to 1925, the real wage in U.S. manufacturing remained relatively constant. Joseph Schumpeter noted:

> Chief of these events was the development of mass production of durables. The purchasing power of American households had to increase at a high rate to keep up with increases in output. The relatively new institution of consumer credit doubtless enabled manufactures to sell their automobiles, radios, and refrigerators in greater volume than would have otherwise been possible. It was necessary, though, that earnings keep up with the increasing output per man-hour of labor-that is, with increasing productivity and the evidence is that they did not. We cannot measure exactly the discrepancy between increases in productivity and increases in real earnings, but in view of the rapid mechanization of industry during the twenties it must have been substantial. Between 1923 and 1929, productivity in the new manufacturing industries may have risen three times as fast as real wages. In any case, it now seems apparent that by the end of the twenties domestic markets were incapable of absorbing the nearly full employment of industry. (Robertson 1973, 669)

The predictions of economic theory in general, and business cycle theory in particular, were not borne out by nominal and real wage developments in the 1920s. Theoretically speaking, a technology shock, by increasing productivity, should raise real wages, by either raising the nominal wage or (and) lowering the price (Shapiro 1987). The data presented above fail to confirm either effect and, more important, provide evidence of wage inertia. Real wages did not increase despite important productivity increases. Further, they raise another, more important question, namely, why did nominal or real wages fail to increase in spite of substantial productivity increases?

3.5.2 Wage and Price Inertia

It is clear that in spite of productivity gains on the order of 62 percent, the nominal wage in manufacturing remained relatively constant. The price level in 1929 was unchanged from 1922. Clearly, wages and prices had not adjusted. Why? Why did wages not increase and prices not decrease? A number of reasons can be offered. For example, it could be argued that the very nature of the technology shock, namely its labor-saving nature, played a crucial role. As had been the case at the Ford Motor Company (FMC), the widespread diffusion of mass production-based production techniques led to an excess-supply of, and not the predicted excess-demand for, labor. Referring to Table 3.7, we see that in 1914, employment at the Ford Motor Company decreased from 14,366 to 12,880, while output increased from 189,088 Model Ts to 230,788. From 1916 to 1928, despite strong growth in total manufacturing output, employment in manufacturing remained constant. In 1916, there were 9,629,000 employees in U.S. manufacturing; in 1928, their number was 9,942,000. Clearly, if anything, the Fordization of U.S. industry, by reducing the demand for labor, put downward pressure on wages.

This brings us to price inertia. Why did prices fail to reflect what were substantial technology-induced cost reductions? At the Ford Motor Company, continuous-flow mass production and the resulting cost savings had led Henry Ford to lower, substantially, the price of Model Ts. Unlike Henry Ford, most managers resisted cost-induced price decreases. The causes of price inertia in this period, I maintain, are numerous. For example, consider the representative producer's decision process as whether or not to adopt continuous-flow mass production techniques (i.e., adopt the production techniques developed at the FMC). Basic investment analysis subsumes constant output and input prices. That is, producers typically assume that prices are exogenously set. It therefore follows that having modernized, managers and shareholders will resist price reductions, as they violate, as it were, the very terms of the implicit contract. For example, price reductions at the Ford Motor Company led shareholders to sue Henry Ford. In 1917, Horace Dodge and John Dodge, two important Ford sub-contractors and shareholders, sued Henry Ford and the Ford Motor Company on the grounds that lower prices for the Model T unfairly decreased dividends and, surprisingly, won.

Another contributing factor is the uncertainty inherent in new technologies. New technologies—in this case, new production processes—such as mass production are unknown entities. As a result, risk-averse, profit-maximizing producers may resist price decreases for fear of either under (or over) estimating cost savings. Uncertainty can as such be considered an important cause of price inertia. Furthermore, since the cost savings in the case of mass production are premised on high volumes, it is not at all clear that at low levels of output (far below rated capacity), producers will be willing to reduce price. Consequently, insufficient demand prevents producers from reducing prices; yet, failure to reduce prices prevents demand from increasing.

Rexford G. Tugwell made a similar argument in 1927. According to biographer Michael Namorato, he felt that:

> Business would only lower prices only when there was a promise of full continuity in the productive process. In light of the individualistic character of American industry, this meant that businessmen reduced prices only if and when they were certain that consumers would buy more of their products and not their competitors. (Namorato 1988, 48)

Thornstein Veblen was more categorical: businessmen, by controlling the rate and volume of output, sabotaged "the productive use of the available industrial plant and workmen":

> Without some salutary restraint in the way of sabotage on the productive use of the available industrial plant and workmen, it is altogether unlikely that prices could be maintained at a reasonably profitable figure for any appreciable time. A businesslike control of the rate and volume of output is indispensable for keeping up a profitable market, and a profitable market is the first and unremitting condition of prosperity in any community whose industry is owned and managed by business men. And the ways and means of this necessary control of the output of industry are always and necessarily something in the way of retardation, restriction, withdrawal, unemployment of plant and workmen-whereby production is kept short of productive capacity. (Veblen 1921, 8)

To Veblen, this amounted to sabotage.

> All this is matter of course, and notorious. But it is not a topic on which one prefers to dwell. Writers and speakers who dilate on the meritorious exploits of the nation's business men will not commonly allude to this voluminous running administration of sabotage, this conscientious withdrawal of efficiency, that goes into their ordinary day's work. (Veblen 1921, 10)

Underlying the sabotage referred to by Veblen was the problem of underincome. Producers, being constrained on product markets, responded by reducing employment (rationalization), or, put differently, by "unmaking markets."

3.5.3 Economic Growth in the 1920's

According to economic growth theory, output and income should grow at a rate of $n + \tau$, where n is the rate of growth of the labor force and τ is the rate of Hicks-neutral or Harrod-neutral technological change. If τ is zero, then the economy will grow at the rate n, the rate of growth of the labor force. If it is positive, then the economy will grow by more than the rate of growth of the labor force. Is there evidence that the U.S. economy grew at abnormally high rates in the 1910s and the 1920s as the result of the electrification of production processes? Did high-throughput, continuous-flow production processes put the U.S. economy on to a higher equilibrium growth path? According to the productivity data presented above, it can be surmised that the relevant values for τ, the Hicks-neutral technology shock, ranged from a low of 1.97 percent in 1926 to a high of 15.31 percent in 1921. For the period 1920–1929, the average rate of labor productivity growth stands at 5.708 percent. The relevant value for n, the average annual rate of labor force growth, when calculated using data from 1910 through 1970, is 1.85 percent. It therefore stands to reason that the average rate of GNP growth in this period is 7.558 percent per annum. Was this the case? Did the U.S. economy grow at an average annual rate of 7.558 percent in the 1920s? Unfortunately, the data fail to provide supporting evidence for this view. Referring to Table 3.11, which presents average rates of growth for given initial and terminal years, we see that U.S. GNP in the 1920s increased at normal—average—rates. For example, for initial years 1918 and 1919, U.S. GNP increased at average annual rates of between 2.7 and 3.4 percent (terminal year, 1929). It is important to point out that in 1920 and 1921, the U.S. economy was in a depression, with GNP having fallen from $151.8 billion in 1918, to $146.4 billion in 1919, $140.0 billion in 1920, and $127.8 billion in 1921.

Table 3.11
Average U.S. GNP Growth Rate

Year	1910	1912	1914	1916	1918	1920
1912	4.1					
1914	1.1	-1.7				
1916	1.9	0.8	3.4			
1918	3.0	2.6	4.9	6.3		
1920	1.5	0.9	1.0	-3.9		
1922	1.8	1.3	2.1	1.6	-0.5	
1924	2.3	2.0	2.8	2.7	1.5	4.3
1926	2.9	2.7	3.5	3.5	2.9	5.2
1928	2.6	2.4	3.0	3.0	2.3	4.0
1930	2.1	1.9	2.4	2.3	1.6	2.7

Source: U.S. Department of Commerce 1975, series F31.

3.5.4 Backward Induction-Based Estimates of Potential U.S. GNP

Estimates of potential GNP play a pivotal role in macroeconomics. For example, they underlie estimates of excess capacity and unemployment, two key macroeconomic variables. Likewise, they provide estimates of forgone opportunities. If the unemployment rate stands at 10 percent, then one can conclude that society has forgone 5 to 10 percent of potential GNP. Not surprisingly, statisticians have developed a number of measures of potential GNP. For example, there potential GNP estimates based on Okun's Law. In the 1960s, Arthur Okun found a relatively stable relationship between output and employment. Specifically, for each percentage point by which the unemployment rate is above the natural rate, real potential GNP is 3 percent below potential GNP. Unemployment and GNP time-series data, it therefore follows, can be used to construct a measure of potential GNP. A second approach consists of simply identifying peaks in actual GNP and joining them with straight lines which serve as measures of potential GNP. The Wharton School Index is one such index.

However, non-negligible problems arise in periods of important technological change. Specifically, both indexes yield biased estimates of potential GNP. For example, the electrification of U.S. industry altered fundamentally the relationship between output and employment. A straight forward application of Okuns law, it therefore follows, will inevitably yield downwardly-biased estimates. The Wharton School Index of potential GNP implicitly assumes that technological change results in an increase in actual GNP. As shown in Chapter 2, private wage and price-setting Nash economies, by their very nature, are unable to make the transition to higher equilibrium growth paths in response to a technology shock. Potential GNP in this case will exceed measured potential GNP.

In view of this, an alternative approach was used, namely, backward extrapolation, which is derived from equilibrium growth theory. As pointed out, economic growth theory maintains that gross national product grows at rate of $n + \tau$, where n is the rate of labor force growth and τ is the rate of Hicks/Harrod-neutral technological change (i.e., measured in terms of productivity). It being the case that positive values of τ are not necessarily translated into contemporaneous output and income growth prevents us from measuring technological change by using actual GNP data for the year(s) in question.

Table 3.12
Backward Extrapolation Estimates of Potential U.S. Gross National Product–Unweighted

	Target Year (t'')		
Base Year (t')	1925	1927	1929
1943	242.32	251.40	260.70
	(.3508)	(.3245)	(.2809)
1944	255.00	264.56	274.40
	(.4216)	(.3938)	(.3164)

One way of getting around this is by assuming that while positive τ's do not result in contemporaneous growth, they do, over time, eventually work themselves into the growth rate, and hence, into actual GNP. It then follows that by identifying such a point in time, estimates of potential GNP for all preceding years can be obtained by extrapolating actual GNP for the year in question backward in time at the rate of growth of the labor supply, hence the nomenclature, backward induction.

For example, suppose that by 1944, the U.S. economy had solved the underlying coordination failure. That is, it had reached its full potential. Potential GNP for the years prior to 1944 can be obtained by simply discounting 1944 actual GNP by the rate of growth of the labor force. In 1944, U.S. GNP stood at $361.3 billion. The rate of growth of the U.S. non-agricultural labor force from

1910 to 1950 was estimated at 1.85 percent per annum. Potential 1925 GNP, it therefore follows, can be obtained by dividing $361.3 billion by 1.4166404 (i.e., 1.018519), the appropriate discount factor, which yields $255.0 billion. Dividing the former by the level of actual 1925 U.S. GNP of $179.4 billion yields a value for τ of 0.4216. That is, the resulting estimate of τ, the technology shock, in this case is 42.1 percent. This approach can also be applied to productivity and wage data. For example, productivity estimates in 1943 relative to 1925 can be used to infer τ values. Similarly, real wage data in 1943 relative to 1925 can be used to infer τ values. Altogether, four techniques were used to estimate potential GNP and t values for the period 1925 to 1944. The first three are based on backward extrapolation, while the fourth simply infers τ values from stock price movements in the 1920s.

Equilibrium Growth Theory-Based Estimates of Potential U.S. GNP

The first set of estimates of potential U.S. GNP and resulting values for τ, the technology shock, was obtained by applying standard growth theory. Growth theory predicts that equilibrium GNP grows at rate $n + τ$ in periods of technological change (Hicks-neutral and Harrod-neutral) and at rate n otherwise, where n is the rate of labor force growth. It therefore follows that by identifying-or assuming-a value for t', the base year, such that the economy finds itself at full employment, potential GNP for all $t < t'$ can be obtained by discounting actual GNP at time t' by a factor $(1+n)$ $t'-t''$, where t'' corresponds to the target year (i.e., the time of the shock). Two base years (i.e., t'), notably 1944 and 1943, and three target years (i.e., t''), 1925, 1927 and 1929, were chosen.

The resulting matrix of potential U.S. GNP values and the corresponding τ values, is provided in Table 3.12. In 1943, real U.S. GNP was 337.1billion (constant 1958 dollars), which, extrapolated backward to1925 at an annual rate of 1.85 percent, yields a value for U.S. GNP in 1925 of 242.3 billion. That is, actual 1925 U.S. GNP of 242.3 billion growing at an annual rate of 1.85 percent, the rate of growth of the labor force, yields a level of 1943 U.S.GNP of $337.1 billion. Dividing this figure by reported actual 1925 GNP of 179.4 billion (constant 1958 dollars) provides a value of τ, the rate of technological change, of 0.3508 (reported in parentheses). By opting for 1944 as the relevant base year, potential 1925 U.S. GNP rises to $255.0 billion, which corresponds to a value for τ of 0.4216.

Taken together, potential U.S. GNP, as defined by the available production technology in 1925 (i.e., mass production), was between 35 (t' = 1943) and 42 (t' = 1944) percent greater than actual GNP. Similarly, potential U.S. GNP in 1927 was between 23 (t' = 1943) and 39 (t' = 1944) percent greater than actual GNP, and lastly, potential GNP in 1929 was between 23 (t' = 1943) and 34 (t' = 1944) percent greater than actual GNP.

Figure 3.3
Actual and Potential GNP 1925-1945

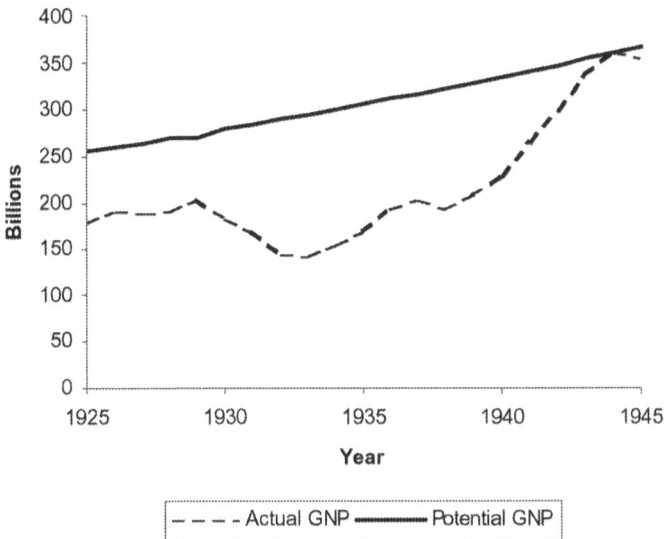

3.5.5 Weighted Estimates

These estimates are based on a number of assumptions, one of which being that the electrification of U.S. industry was instantaneous; that is, the process innovations developed at Ford's Highland Park plant were instantaneously diffused throughout all sectors of the U.S. economy. Clearly, this is a strong assumption. It is a well-known fact that with all process innovations, major or minor, there are significant diffusion lags. Producers may delay the application of the new technology to coincide with their investment cycle. Or conversely, they may find themselves constrained on product markets, which will also lead to delays. Thus, it would be naive to assume that mass production instantaneously revolutionized U.S. industry. A more reasonable view would be that it altered productivity and output over a period of time. In light of this, I generated a second set of estimates of potential GNP and τ, the technology shock. Using the electrification diffusion index found in Beaudreau (1996a), we derived the matrix of weighted potential U.S. GNP values and τ values provided in Table 3.12. Specifically, the estimates of τ obtained in Table 3.12 were simply scaled by a diffusion index. For example, unweighted potential 1925 U.S. GNP stands at $255.0 billion, which yields a τ value of 0.4216. By 1925, electrification had penetrated roughly 47.7 percent of producers in the U.S. manufacturing sector. Multiplying the former by the latter results in a weighted estimate of τ of 0.20. Substantially lower estimates of potential GNP and τ now result. For example, weighted potential GNP in 1925 (base year 1944) stands at $215.5 billion ($\tau$ =.2013) as opposed to $255.0 billion ($\tau$ = .4216). In general, potential U.S. GNP, as defined by the production technology in place in 1925 (i.e., mass production), was between 16.7 (t' = 1943) and 20.1 (t' = 1944) percent greater than actual GNP. Moreover, potential U.S. GNP in 1927 was between 19.7 (t' = 1943) and 24.2 (t' = 1944) percent greater than actual GNP, and lastly, potential GNP in 1929 was between 17.2 (t' = 1943) and 21.4 (t' = 1944) percent greater than actual GNP.

Table 3.13
Backward Extrapolation Estimates of Potential U.S. Gross National Product–Weighted

	Target Year (t'')		
Base Year (t')	1925	1927	1929
1943	209.4	227.3	238.8
	(.1675)	(.1979)	(.1729)
1944	215.5	235.3	247.2
	(.2013)	(.2402)	(.2141)

Source: Beaudreau (1996), 93.

3.5.6 Henry Ford, Edward A. Filene and Underincome

Given the nature of the technology shock (i.e. electrification), it could be argued that those most likely to be aware of the problem of underincome—income inertia—would be those closest to it (i.e. the technology shock). Those choosing not to convert to continuous-flow mass production would, it therefore follows, be least aware, and vice-versa. As it turns out, history bears this out, as Henry Ford, the founder and president of the Ford Motor Company, was among the first to identify and, more importantly, act on the problem of underincome. Throughout the 1910's, 1920's, and 1930's, Ford pointed repeatedly to the problem of underincome (nominal and real) as a structural weakness in the U.S. economy. For example, at a 1929 conference at the White House with President Hoover, Ford recommended:

> …increasing the purchasing power of our principal customers The American People…this can be done in two ways: first, by putting additional value into goods or reducing prices to the level of actual values; and second, starting a movement to increase the general wage level. Nearly everything in this country is too high priced. The only thing that should be high priced in this country is the man who works. Wages must not come down, they must not even stay at their present level; they must go up. (Fisher 1930, 25)

Later, in 1933, throwing his support behind the National Industrial Recovery Act of 1933 (NIRA), Ford declared:

> We've got to stop that gouging process if we want to see all of the people reasonably prosperous. There is only one rule for industrialists and that is: Make the best quality of goods possible at the lowest cost paying the highest wages possible. Nothing can be right in this country until wages are right. The life of business comes forth from the people in orders. The factories are not stopped for lack of money but for lack of orders. Money loaned at the top means nothing. Money spent at the bottom starts everything. I think that if industrial leaders had been willing to push wages up and up during the last thirty years the present economic ills would at least not be as great as they are. If the government can help in these matters, well and good, but the government has not a rosy record in running itself thus far. (*New York Times*, June 16, 1933, 2)

Ford practiced what he preached. On January 17, 1914, the Board of Directors of the Ford Motor Company approved a new wage scale which doubled wages from the plant average of $2.50 per day to $5.00. This was followed by the six-dollar day in 1919 and the seven-dollar day in 1932. Throughout this period, the price of Ford products, notably the Model T, decreased monotonically. For example in 1909, the sticker price was $950.00; by 1916, it had fallen 62 percent to $360.00.

The five-dollar day earned Ford the wrath of the business community in the greater Detroit area and throughout the country. Irresponsible, illogical, and folly were some of the adjectives used to describe both Ford and the five-dollar day. A small minority, however, saw Ford as an visionary businessman. One such person was Boston merchant Edward A. Filene, who, throughout this period, argued the virtues of Ford-inspired mass production and mass distribution.

> In the future a really big business success on the basis of mass production and mass distribution will be impossible except as it makes for both high wages and low prices… Low wages and high prices manifestly cut down that widespread and sustained buying power of the masses without which mass production sooner or later defeats itself. In other words, the business man of the future must produce prosperous customers as well as saleable goods. He cannot think of business as an adventure in getting money from the masses of people who, in one way or another for which he has no responsibility, have got money from someone else. His whole business policy must look forward to creating great buying power among the masses. Otherwise mass production cannot succeed. The business man of the future must fill the pockets of the workers and consumers before he can fill his pockets. (Filene 1924, 201)

Sensing resistance from both the business and academic communities, Filene attempted a foray into the world of political economy, publishing a paper in the *American Economic Review* in 1923 entitled "The Minimum Wage and Efficiency," in which he formalized Ford's call for higher wages into a minimum-wage argument. Not surprisingly, his career was short-lived. He subsequently turned to writing books (e.g. *The Way Out: A Forecast of Coming Changes in American Business, and Successful Living in This Machine Age*). Like Robert Owen a century earlier, Ford and Filene set their sights high: reform the for-profit economy, and, in the process, release the potential energy deepening had conferred on the United Kingdom, and the United States.

3.5.7 Steam Power and Electric Power: A Study in Contrasts

Despite the many similarities, the first and second industrial revolutions differed in many regards, some of which are noteworthy. Take, for example, their effect on product prices. Referring to Table 3.5, we see that throughout the early 1800's, prices of manufactures, denoted here as *Industry*, decreased monotonically, going from 198 in 1810 to 112 in 1871. This stands in stark contrast with the price of manufactures in the United States in the 1920's, as shown in Table 3.9. As Thornstein Veblen had put it, American manufacturers resisted price decreases, despite substantially lower costs.

This raises the question why? Why did energy deepening-based capacity increases lead to lower prices in the United Kingdom, but not in the United States? The answer, I believe, is twofold, involving the structure of industry, and, secondly, the market for feed-stocks (e.g. raw cotton in the case of the U.K.). Specifically, the cotton industry in 18th century Great Britain was highly competitive, owing to the absence of entry barriers. The data bear this out. For example, in the town of Manchester. This stands in contrast with U.S. industry which was more concentrated. The quintessential example is the Ford Motor Company which controlled 85 percent of the automobile market. The second factor is the nature of the market for feed-stocks. The supply of raw cotton increased dramatically in the early 19th century. This, as it turns out, put downward pressure on price, as seen in Table 3.4. With cotton arriving from abroad in record quantities, and prices falling, the temptation to try one's hand at making cloth was, for many budding industrialists, too hard to pass up. Record amounts of cloth were produced, forcing prices down.

Such was not the case in U.S. manufacturing where, often times, downstream producers controlled upstream suppliers.

3.5.8 Policy Responses

As I have argued here and elsewhere (Beaudreau 1996a), the electrification of U.S. industry throughout the early 20th century created a gap between actual output and potential output. With what was essentially the same capital and labor, U.S. producers could increase output by increasing throughput rates, as seen at the Ford Motor Company. According to Alfred Chandler Jr.:

> In modern mass production, as in modern mass distribution and modern transportation and communications, economies resulted more from sped than size. It was not the size of the manufacturing establishment in terms of the number of workers and the amount and value of productive equipment, but the velocity of throughput and the resulting increase in volume that permitted economies that lowered costs and increases output per worker and machine. (Chandler 1977, 327)

The U.S. government, defined widely to include the executive, the legislative and the judicial, I argue, was not oblivious to this. Senators, representatives, presidents, and cabinet members throughout this period referred to overcapacity (overproduction, underconsumption) in myriad ways, not knowing exactly how to describe it. Examples.

Like the government of Sir Robert Peel in 19th-century Great Britain, succes-
sive U.S. governments were called upon to "do something." As I argued in Beaudreau (1996a), the government responded in two ways, first by way of
commercial policy (Smoot-Hawley Tariff Bill of 1929), and second, with the
National Industrial Recovery Act of 1933. Both were responses to the underlying
problem of underincome.

The problem as I have shown was the failure on the part of producers to
increase income commensurately with potential output. Merchants, as was
shown, have no incentives to increase orders of consumption and capital goods,
resulting in inertia. The question, therefore, was how to increase the demand, on
the part of merchants, for U.S. consumption and capital goods? As the analysis
presented in Chapter 2 shows, the only bona fide way is for producers to increase
operating capital, via wage increases, thus prompting merchants to increase
orders of consumption and capital goods. Senator Reed Smoot of Utah, chairman of the Senate Finance Committee, was aware of this. According to biographer Milton Merrill:

> On his return to Utah in August 1932, in preparation for his final battle in
> political life, Smoot advised his people that it had been the common attitude
> in 1930 to attribute the depression to unwise governmental policies, with the
> Smoot-Hawley act specified. Lest there were some obsessed with heresy, he
> declared, "To hold the American tariff policy, or any other policy of out gov-
> ernment, responsible for this gigantic deflationary move is only to display
> one's ignorance of its sweeping universal character. The world is paying for its
> ruthless destruction of life and property in the World War and for its failure
> to adjust purchasing power to productive capacity during the industrial revo-
> lution of the decade following the war." (Merrill 1990, 340)

Interestingly, Smoot chose commercial policy over income policy to deal with
the problem of underincome. Alleging increased and increasing imports of manufactures and foodstuffs in the mid-to-late 1920s as the principal cause of U.S.
industry's woes, he along with the Republican party called for yet another
upward revision of tariff schedules.

On July 28, 1928, Senator Reed Smoot officially unveiled the economic plank
of Republican presidential hopeful Herbert C. Hoovers election platform. Tariffs
on both agricultural and manufactured goods would be raised and taxes would be
lowered.[6] The New York Times reported:

Upward revision of the tariff and another reduction in taxes by the next Congress if Secretary Hoover is elected President were predicted today by Senator Smoot, Chairman of the Finance Committee. Senator Smoot, who, as Chairman of the Resolutions Committee at the Kansas City Convention, drafted the tariff plank, said today that the Republican Party in this plank had promised not only upward revision of the industrial schedules but assured the farmers that the agricultural schedules would be raised to prevent the increasing importations of farm products.[7]

The underlying logic is easily understood in terms of the model of producer-merchant exchange presented in Chapter 2. One way to increase U.S. merchants' orders of from domestic producers is by decreasing their orders from foreign producers. One way to do this is by imposing restrictive tariffs, making foreign goods more costly—in this case, prohibitively more costly. Clearly, this is a naive strategy, especially in light of foreign retaliation. Nonetheless, it was the policy that the U.S. government chose, the bill being signed into law on June 17, 1930.

It is important to point out, however, that opinions were divided, even in the Republican party. The most telling example is the growing rift between Old-Guard Republicans, Smoot included, and President Herbert Hoover. It is fair to say that, political ambitions aside, Hoover was against raising tariffs. In his view, the problem confronting the U.S. economy was the lack of income. Income would have to rise, he maintained. To this end, producers would have to voluntarily cooperate, raising wages, and lowering prices. This he defined as the associative state. Clearly, Hoover knew better than his party. Higher tariffs would, in the long run, do nothing to resolve the problem of underincome.

While a disgruntled Hoover would go on to defeat in the 1932 presidential election, his idea of the associative state, based on industrial self-discipline, would live on, being the cornerstone of the National Industrial Recovery Act of 1933 (NIRA), the Roosevelt administration's policy response to the Great Depression. The NIRA called for higher wages, stable prices, and a reduction in the work week, not to mention the right for workers to bargain collectively. Based on the writings of Columbia University professor Rexford G. Tugwell, the NIRA sought to increase wages and, consequently, consumption. According to Tugwell, the "second industrial revolution" had increased output, income and profits, but left wage income, the main determinant of consumption, unchanged. In other words, the new technology had passed labor by, resulting in a more skewed functional distribution of income.

The picture of the modern industrial situation which must be carried in any honest and informed mind is one of a very mixed sort. Technique itself is having certain clear evolutionary movements. The main one, to which attention has been called here, is that of a double concentration and elaborative process. But this process has not been carried forward evenly. And it has built up new social groups which, while they exploited its new possibilities, have clung dogmatically to the theory of an outworn system of institutions. This happens, of course, because the active exploiters found that so long as the public could be persuaded to keep its eyes on an idealized picture, their own real activities, not being understood, could go on without much if any hampering control. Incidentally, this lack of control has made it possible for them to divert to their own uses, the greater share of the increased economic surpluses created by the new improvements. (Tugwell 1933, 85)

As I pointed out in Beaudreau (1996a), the evidence does not support this view. The functional distribution of income, as reported by Keller (1973) and U.S. Department of Commerce (1975), was relatively stable in the 1920s. As predicted by the theory of underincome, aggregate income cannot increase in response to a paradigm technology shock, for lack of private incentives to increase wage income, profit income being a residual. Senator Reed Smoot, Rexford G. Tugwell, and the architects of the National Industrial Recovery Act, including the celebrated Brains' Trust, were unaware of this. However, it need be pointed out that Tugwell and Harold Moulton, director of the Brookings Institution, came surprisingly close to uncovering the problem of underincome as described above. In their view, cooperation would have to replace competition.

3.5.9 Other Policy Prescriptions

The set of policy prescriptions in the 1930s was exceedingly wide, and included Thornstein Veblen's notion of a new social order in which businessmen would be replaced by engineers and the abandonment of the for-profit economy, Technocracy, based on the writings of Walter Rautenstrauch and Howard Scott, and social credit, based on the ideas of Clifford H. Douglas. It is my contention that, like the Smoot-Hawley Tariff Act of 1930 and the National Industrial Recovery Act of 1933, each of these constitutes a response to underincome. The problem, however, is that not one is able to identify the underlying problem, namely the absence of private incentives on the part of producers to increase income in response to a technology shock, in a world in which profits are a residual form of income. Lacking then, as today, was an empirically-consistent model of producer-merchant exchange. As was pointed out in Beaudreau (1999), only Douglas attempted to model exchange, with mixed results.

3.5.10 Underincome and Early 20th-Century Political Economy

As I argued in Beaudreau (1999a), the Great Depression rekindled the debates among political economists that had characterized the early 19th century. Were underconsumption and unemployment chronic in private, competitive economies? Would markets, specifically, wage and price adjustment, restore full employment and economic growth?

There were, however, some important differences. First, non-mainstream theories were now more sophisticated. Writers like Stuart Chase and Howard Scott pointed to, in unequivocal terms, energy deepening in the form of electrification as the principal cause of the Great Depression (Chase 1934, Scott 1933). This owed, in large measure, to the development of thermodynamics, the science of heat and work. Contrast this with the early-19th century, where steam power, or "fire power" as Adam Smith referred to it, was an unknown entity. Robert Owen, for example, referred to it as "scientific power." Another important difference were the many 19th-century developments in price theory. Alfred Marshall's Principles of Economics, published in 1890, contributed to a better understanding of markets among early 20th century political economists, as well as a better reference point for critics like Thornstein Veblen. That prices failed to decrease in response to cost-decreasing innovations (electrification) is what led Thornstein Veblen to condemn the "for-profit" economy, and call for its replacement by output-maximizing engineers.

3.6 Post-World War II Energy Deepening

While World War II allowed the U. S. economy to realize the potential that had been building (accumulating) for over three decades, it did not, unfortunately, mark the end of energy deepening-based underincome. Cast in terms of growth theory, World War II, by contributing to higher overall expenditure and real wages, pushed the U.S. economy on to the growth path defined by three decades of energy deepening. The problem, however, was that, by 1946, the equilibrium growth path had, once again, migrated upwards, the result of further energy deepening. In the decade from 1945 to 1955, total industrial consumption of electric power more-than-doubled going from 146,261 million kilowatt hours in

1945 to 334 to 334,088 million kilowatt hours. From 1955 to 1965, it increased by another 60 percent. By 1965, the United States consumed more electric power than all other countries combined. Never before in the history of mankind had per-capita energy consumption increased so rapidly.

This "energy orgy" came to a sudden, unexpected end with the oil/energy crisis in the 1970's. Responding to the falling real oil prices, members of the Organization of Petroleum Exporting Countries (OPEC) provoked an artificial crisis in 1973, resulting in the quadrupling of oil and other energy prices. With this came the end of what had been over a century of declining real energy prices (Jorgenson 1983). Per-worker energy consumption, monotone increasing for most of this century, stopped rising, resulting in the end of conventionally-defined productivity growth, and the onset of an era of growth and productivity slowdown.

This section examines post-World War II energy deepening in three countries, the United States, Germany, and Japan, with the focus on manufacturing. It will be argued that unlike energy deepening in the 19th and early 20th centuries which resulted in underincome and stagnation, energy deepening in this period resulted in three decades of unprecedented and uninterrupted growth, a sort of golden era of economic growth. This raises a number of questions, notably, why did energy deepening in this period differ from energy deepening in the past? After all, it was a continuation of the process of energy deepening begun with the steam engine in the late 18th century. The difference, I argue, lies with the exchange technology, specifically with a number of New Deal-based changes in the process of income creation. First, there was the Wagner Act of 1935 which allowed for the creation of unions and collective bargaining. As a result, wages (nominal and real) would now track productivity. Second, governments, by way of John M. Keynes' General Theory reentered the business of "making markets," a business they had abandoned—although not completely—in the 19th century. In short, while unaware of it, the architects of the New Deal had solved the problem of underincome.

3.6.1 The Evidence for U.S., German and Japanese Manufacturing

The analysis here differs markedly from that of the previous two sections. Instead of using various proxies for energy consumption and productivity growth, growth accounting techniques are used. Specifically, a version of the KLEMS production function, developed by Ernst Berndt and David O. Wood, is used to estimate the contribution of energy-related and organization-related factor inputs to output growth (Berndt and Wood 1975; Beaudreau 1995).

The KLEP Production Function

To evaluate the contribution of electric power, conventionally-defined labor and capital to manufacturing output growth in the United States, Germany and Japan, I proceeded to estimate the KLEP (capital, labor, and electric power) production function. Specifically, I assumed the existence of a well-behaved, twice differentiable, monotonic and quasi-concave production function, such as (1), where Q = value added, EP = electric power, L = employment, and K = capital. Christensen and Jorgenson (1970) and Gollop and Jorgenson (1980) define the rate of growth of total factor productivity, $tfp = dTFP/dt \, 1/TFP$, as $tfp = q - s_{EP} \, ep - s_K \, k - s_L \, l$, where $q = dQ/dt \, 1/Q$, $ep = dEP/dt \, 1/EP$, $k = dK/dt \, 1/K$, $l = dL/dt \, 1/L$ and s_i is the weighted average of the ith factor share over the discrete time interval $\forall \, i = EP, L, K$ (Gullickson and Harper 1988).

$$Q_t = f[EP_t, L_t, K_t] \tag{3.4}$$

For the reasons described in Beaudreau (1995,1998), the relevant factor-input elasticities were estimated directly (i.e. as opposed to indirectly using the cost function). Specifically, data on value added, electric power consumption, total employment and capital for U.S., German and Japanese manufacturing were used to estimate the Cobb-Douglas KLEP production function:

$$Q_t = EP_t^{\,\beta 1} \, L_t^{\,\beta 2} \, K_t^{\,\beta 3}. \tag{3.5}$$

Estimates for these output elasticities for the three countries are presented in Table 3.14. What is particularly noteworthy are the similarities. In all three cases, electric power consumption is, by far, the most important factor input, as evidenced by factor elasticities of 0.537244, 0.747482 and 0.605599. Similarly, labor and capital are marginally important, confirming the results obtained in Chapter 4.

The Productivity Slowdown: Evidence from U.S., German and Japanese Manufacturing

As it turns, these estimates and the resulting fixed-weight factor input indexes did more than confirm the historical view of the role of energy in output and productivity growth: they provided the wherewithal to reexamine the energy-productivity slowdown debate (Jorgenson 1983). Further, they showed that the commonly-used factor shares provide severely biased estimates of output elasticities.

Table 3.14
KLEP Output Elasticities: U.S., German and Japanese Manufacturing

Inputs	U.S. 1950–1984	Germany 1963–1988	Japan 1965–1988
EP	0.537244	0.747482	0.605599
	(26.551)	(3.135)	(3.017)
L	0.399727	0.121134	0.197653
	(18.231)	(2.332)	(1.847)
K	0.075049	0.131383	0.196748
	(2.768)	(0.543)	(1.608)
Constant	0.075049	0.046106	-0.019274
	(9.956)	(1.426)	(0.271)
R^2	0.98438	0.95821	0.98314
F	1008.5140	229.2853	612.1780

The Growth Slowdown

Table 3.15 reports the relevant growth rates for manufacturing value added (Q), electric power (EP), labor (L) and capital (K), as well as the relevant fixed-weight index for aggregate inputs (AI) (Hisnanick and Kymm 1992; Gullickson and Harper 1988) for three time intervals: 1950–1984, 1950–1973, and 1974–1984.

Unlike most studies which point to the existence of a sizable gap between the actual rates of growth of output and aggregate input (i.e. the Solow residual), these results show that growth in U.S., German and Japanese manufacturing value added is fully explained by growth in the relevant fixed-weight factor-input growth indexes. For the complete period 1950–1984, U.S. manufacturing value added increased at an average annual rate of 2.684 percent, while the aggregate input increased at 2.655 percent. For the first sub-period 1950–1973, it increased at 3.469, while the aggregate input increased at 3.466 percent. In the second sub-period, 1974–1984, it increased at an average annual rate of 0.121, while the aggregate input increased at 0.310.

Chief among the causes of growth in U.S., German and Japanese manufacturing value added is electric power consumption. In the U.S. case, electric power consumption increased at an average annual rate of 4.052 percent over the period 1950–1984. Specifically, U.S. per worker consumption of electric power in this period goes from 12,534 kilowatt hours in 1950 to 41,688 kilowatt hours in 1984, a total increase of 232 percent [U.S. Department of Commerce (various years)]. When multiplied by the relevant output elasticity (i.e. 0.537244), the growth in electric power consumption in U.S. manufacturing accounts for 82 percent of overall output growth (i.e. 2.17/2.68), which corroborates the predictions of the energy-organization approach to production analysis. Prior to the energy crisis (i.e. 1973), electric power consumption in manufacturing increased at an average annual rate of 5.371 percent. Output increased at an average annual rate of 3.466 percent. Electric power consumption growth, it then follows, accounts for 83 percent of output growth (i.e. 2.88/3.46). In the post-energy-crisis period, electric power consumption increased at an average annual rate of 0.246, while output increased at an average annual rate of 0.121.

Table 3.15
Output and Input Growth Rates: U.S., German and Japanese Manufacturing

U.S.

	1950–1984	1950–1973	1974–1984
USV A	2.684	3.469	0.121
USAI*	2.674	3.472	0.310
USEP	4.052	5.371	0.246
USN	0.662	0.900	-0.091
USK	3.694	3.614	3.4008

Germany

	1963–1988	1962–1973	1974–1988
GERV A	2.462	6.522	1.486
GERAI*	2.433	5.190	1.080
GEREP	2.894	5.883	1.366
GERN	-0.785	0.592	-0.938
GERK	2.945	5.620	1.406

Japan

	1965–1988	1965–1973	1974–1988
JAPVA	3.826	8.844	3.099
JAPAI*	3.566	9.858	1.538
JAPEP	3.559	11.320	0.965
JAPN	-0.082	2.297	-0.367
JAPK	7.520	13.536	5.182

The Productivity Slowdown

Gullickson and Harper (1988) and Hisnanick and Kymm (1992) evaluate the sources of productivity growth in U.S. manufacturing using $lp = q - l$ (see Equation 3.6) as the appropriate measure of labor productivity.[10] In this section, I report a series of revised estimates of the role of electric power and capital in labor productivity in U.S., German and Japanese manufacturing. Referring to Table 3.16, we see that the rate of growth of labor productivity is, in all three cases, entirely explained by increasing electric power and capital intensities, defined here as $ep - l$, the shift away from labor to electric power, and $k - l$, the shift away from labor to capital.

$$lp = q - l = \beta_1 [ep - l] + \beta_3 [k - l] + tfp \qquad (3.6)$$

In the U.S. case, over the entire sample period (i.e. 1950–1984), labor productivity increased at an average annual rate of 2.022 percent. During this period, the electric power-labor ratio increased at an average annual rate of 3.39 percent, which when multiplied by the relevant elasticity (i.e. 0.537244), yields a value of 1.820 percent, which measures the effects on labor productivity of the substitution of labor for electric power referred to by Dale Jorgenson (Jorgenson (1988)). Also, during this period, the capital-labor ratio increased at an average annual rate of 3.032, which when multiplied by the relevant elasticity yields a value of 0.191, which measures the effects on labor productivity of the substitution of labor for capital. The sum of these two effects account for 99.5 percent of the growth in labor productivity in U.S. manufacturing.

Prior to the energy crisis, labor productivity increased at an average annual rate of 2.569 percent, of which 2.400 percent can be attributed to labor-electric power substitution and 0.170 percent can be attributed to labor-capital substitution. Together, these two effects overstate the overall increase in labor productivity by 1 percent. In the ensuing decade, labor productivity increased at an average annual rate of 0.212 percent, of which 0.180 percent can be attributed to labor-electric power substitution and 0.219 percent can be attributed to labor-capital substitution.

Table 3.16
Productivity Growth: U.S., German and Japanese Manufacturing

U.S.

	1950–1984	1950–1973	1974–1984
uslp	2.022	2.569	0.212
ustfp	0.010	-0.007	-0.1889
$\hat{\beta}_1(usep - usn)$	1.820	2.400	0.180
$\beta_3(usk - usn)$	0.191	0.170	0.219

Germany

	1963–1988	1963–1973	1974–1988
gerlp	3.247	5.930	2.424
gertfp	0.007	1.315	0.3942
$\beta_1(gerep - gern)$	2.750	3.954	1.722
$\beta_3(gerk - gern)$	0.489	0.660	0.307

Japan

	1965–1988	1965–1973	1974-1988
japlp	3.908	6.547	3.466
japtfp	0.208	-1.126	1.567
$\beta_1(japep - japn)$	2.204	5.469	0.806
$\beta_3(japk - japn)$	1.495	2.210	1.091

3.6.2 The Problem of Underincome

This brings us to the question of underincome, specifically, given the unprecedented rates of energy deepening in this period, why was it not characterized by recessions and depressions? After all, the values for α in U.S., German, and Japanese manufacturing industries were increasing at unprecedented rates. All of the necessary conditions, as dictated by history (first and second industrial revolutions), were in place.

The answer to this question lies in the various developments in the 1930's, specifically, in the advent of collective bargaining and the rise of Keynesian economics, with its emphasis on macroeconomic stabilization through government expenditure. I begin with collective bargaining. The Wagner Act of 1935 and the resulting National Labor Relations Bureau did more than increase labor's bargaining power vis-à-vis capital, it almost single-handedly solved the problem of underincome. Theoretically, ω_{ic}, consumption good producer i's demand for operating capital was, in the presence of productivity-based collective bargaining, tied to α, the productivity of labor (or conversely, the productivity of operating capital). In times of energy deepening (higher electric power consumption per worker), wages would increase, as would individual producer working capital, and, at the aggregate level, overall working capital (national income), prompting merchants to increase their demand for consumption and capital goods, and, in the process, providing the wherewithal for a successful transition to the new, higher equilibrium growth path defined by the technology shock.

In short, the nominal and real wage inertia that had characterized early 19th century Great Britain, and early 20th-century America was eliminated. Nominal and real wages would, from this point on, be tied to productivity growth, which, in turn, was tied to energy consumption growth.

Table 3.17
Value Added and Earnings Per Production Worker U.S. Manufacturing
1958-1993

Year	PW*	VAPW**	SALPW*	Ratio
1958	11,681	12,308	4,246	0.345
1959	12,272	13,152	4,388	0.333
1960	12,209	13,206	4,404	0.333
1961	11,778	13,547	4,445	0.328
1962	12,126	14,177	4,609	0.325
1963	12,232	14,874	4,735	0.318
1964	12,403	15,510	4,878	0.314
1965	13,076	15,873	4,921	0.310
1966	13,826	16,150	4,969	0.307
1967	13,955	16,189	4,959	0.306
1968	14,041	16,833	5,094	0.302
1969	14,357	16,759	5,073	0.302
1970	13,528	16,665	5,008	0.300
1971	12,874	17,582	5,135	0.292
1972	13,527	18,253	5,353	0.293
1973	14,232	18,720	5,373	0.287
1974	13,927	19,275	5,226	0.271
1975	12,568	19,224	5,155	0.268
1976	13,052	20,242	5,317	0.262
1977	13,691	20,759	5,440	0.262
1978	14,228	20,867	5,458	0.261
1979	14,537	20,864	5,249	0.251
1980	13,900	18,793	4,968	0.264
1981	13,542	20,124	4,948	0.245
1982	12,400	20,433	4,914	0.240
1983	12,203	21,514	5,018	0.233
1984	12,572	22,322	5,097	0.228
1985	12,174	22,627	5,169	0.228
1986	11,765	23,573	5,230	0.221
1987	12,242	24,677	5,176	0.209
1988	12,404	25,330	5,165	0.203
1989	12,341	25,248	5,070	0.200
1990	12,128	24,978	4,995	0.199
1991	11,513	25,096	4,959	0.197
1992	11,648	26,098	5,029	0.019
1993	11,731	26,233	4,999	0.190

*'000
**Constant 1958 dollars

3.6.3 Productivity and Earnings in U.S. Manufacturing 1958–1973: Evidence

As shown in Table 3.17, U.S. manufacturing value added per production worker increased monotonically from 1958 to 1993. Table 3.16 presents U.S. manufacturing value added per production worker (VAPW) from 1958 to 1993, earnings per production worker (SALPW), and the ratio of the latter to the former. We see that from 1958 to 1993, manufacturing value added per production worker increased monotonically; however, compensation per production worker increased monotonically from 1958 to 1973, but remained stable from 1974 to 1993.

3.6.4 Government Expenditure

Productivity-based collective bargaining, I maintain, is a sufficient condition to resolve the problem of income inertia (underincome). Accordingly, greater energy consumption would lead, automatically, to higher real wages, which, in turn, would increase producers' demand for operating capital and merchants' demand for operating capital and goods and services. In the end, output, income and expenditure would increase in tandem, making for a successful transition. Another possibility, as pointed out in Chapter 2, is central bank-financed government expenditure, with concomitant taxation. Here, governments would finance their expenditure at the central bank—or private bank—and proceed to place orders for goods and services. Merchants would, in turn, increase their demand for goods and services—and credit—from producers. The key requirement here, however, is that the government finance its expenditure via newly issued credit. Government expenditure financed in capital markets will, it only follows, crowd out private expenditure, and, hence, not give rise to an increase in income (operating capital, credit). Similarly, government expenditure financed by income taxation will crowd out private expenditure, and, hence, fail to increase overall income.

These results have important implications for Keynesian macroeconomic policy, notably with regard to their efficacy. Unless overall credit (working capital) increases, government expenditure is neutral in so far as output and employment are concerned. As pointed out in Beaudreau (1996a), the Roosevelt Administration's profit tax in 1936 was an inappropriate policy measure given the underlying problem, namely underincome.

3.6.5 Other Contributing Factors

Another important contributing factor in the resolution of the problem of under-income in the post-WWII period was the development of consumer credit. By definition, consumer credit consists of a financial instrument, created by either a financial or non-financial institution, which (*i*) increases the overall level of outstanding credit, and (*ii*) is unrelated to aggregate savings. That is, it is unrelated to the level of savings at any given point in time. Formally, consumer credit increases the level of outstanding level of credit, and, as such, money income.

Technically, consumer credit is analogous to bank credit issued to either producers or merchants. The relevant institution obtains credit from the banking sector, uses it to extend credit to its clients, and then proceeds to sell the resulting claim (liability) to the financial sector. The resulting revenues are then used to retire the outstanding bank liability.

The 20th century witnessed the emergence of and large-scale use of consumer credit. Banks, producers, and merchants began issuing credit, increasing the overall level of money income, and, in the process, closing the gap between actual income and potential income. Large-scale producers, such as General Motors, Ford, Chrysler, Westinghouse, and General Electric established credit divisions, the most successful of which has been General Electric Credit Corporation.

Table 3.18 presents time-series data on aggregate outstanding consumer credit in the United States. We see that consumer credit, as an institution, literally took off in the post-WWII period, doubling between 1946 and 1949. From 1901 to 1945, it increased roughly 470 percent, while from 1945 to 1968, it increased some 1,885 percent.

Table 3.18
Consumer Credit, United States, 1901-1968

Year	Credit
1901	1.0
1912	2.0
1922	5.7
1929	8.6
1933	4.3
1939	7.8
1945	5.8
1946	8.5
1947	11.8
1948	14.7
1949	17.6
1950	21.8
1951	23.1
1952	27.9
1953	31.8
1954	32.9
1955	39.4
1956	43.1
1957	45.9
1958	46.1
1959	51.5
1960	56.1
1961	58.0
1962	63.8
1963	71.7
1964	80.3
1965	90.3
1966	97.5
1967	102.1
1968	113.2

*Billions
Source: U.S. Department of Commerce 1975, Series F387.

3.6.6. The Energy Crisis and the Productivity Slowdown

The energy crisis of the 1970's (1973 and 1979) brought an end to what has to rank as the golden-age of material civilization in the West, namely the post-World War II period from 1945 to 1975. Throughout this period, energy deepening in the form of rising electric power consumption growth rates led, invariably, to rising output and productivity rates. The energy crisis, by quadrupling the price of energy, put an end to this. Since then, output has grown at one-third to one-half the previous rate, and, more importantly, productivity has been flat.

There was, however, an upside, as far as the problem of underincome is concerned. Specifically, the end of energy deepening brought with it the end of the problem of underincome. Potential output would, hitherto, grow at the rate of growth of the labor force.

With the threat gone, the policy tools referred to above no longer had their raison d'être, which explains, in large measure, the demise of collective bargaining and government expenditure since. Labor union membership has declined monotonically since the early 1980's. Government expenditure, as a percentage of GDP, has also declined. One could argue that, in the absence of the problem of underincome, neither no longer has its historical role to play of "making the market," or "helping make the market."

The question it therefore follows is whether Western industrialized nations are now immune to the problem of underincome, given the end of energy deepening? In the next chapter, I examine a second type of underincome, namely non-energy-deepening based underincome, where underincome results not from an increase in productive capacity—as was the case throughout the 19th and 20th centuries—but from a decrease in overall operating capital (i.e. ω), brought about by organization-related technology shocks. Foremost among these is the substitution of animate forms of supervision (workers) by inanimate forms (sensors, computers, control devices). For example, replacing a worker by a machine will reduce ω_{ic} at the producer level. If enough producers adopt the new technology, then the specter of underincome arises.

3.7 Conclusions

As was demonstrated formally in Chapter 2, organized trade, in general, is not spontaneous. Markets do not emerge spontaneously, and, more importantly, income, the wherewithal of trade, does not increase spontaneously—that is, off-of the relevant growth path. Prisoner's dilemmas and indeterminacies abound, making for a situation in which the potential for trade is not a sufficient condition for actual trade to occur. Put differently, greater productive capacity is not a sufficient condition for greater output, income and expenditure.

This chapter focused on the problem of income inertia—underincome—in the presence of energy deepening. Two cases of energy deepening were considered, namely the development and application of the steam engine in the United Kingdom in the 19th century, and the development and application of electric power in the United States in the 20th century. It was shown that while the steam engine increased Great Britain's capacity to transform fibers into thread and thread into cloth, and iron ore into steel and steel into finished products, income, the wherewithal of trade in a market setting, did not increase commensurately, resulting in recurrent commercial crises. Income inertia aborted the transition to a new higher equilibrium growth path, leaving, in its wake, unemployment, falling prices and wages, and poverty in the midst of plenty. The same scenario played itself out in the 20th century with the development and application of electric power in the United States.

Put differently, man's scientific genius fell victim to the inertia that is the hallmark of social relationships, the same inertia that had, for millennia, prevented the spontaneous emergence of organized exchange, and, ultimately, free markets. Man's grasp, however, exceeded his reach, the latter being constrained by prisoner's dilemmas. While science had provided the blueprint for a brave new world of unlimited wealth (*Unbound Prometheus*), based on increasing energy consumption, Western nations, specifically the United Kingdom and the United States, were unable to execute it.

As had been the case throughout the history of trade and exchange, government, defined here any form of coordination or cooperation, provided the wherewithal to overcome this inertia. The National Regeneration Society, the Repeal of the Corn Laws, the Fordney-McCumber Tariff Act of 1922, the Smoot-Hawley Tariff Act of 1930, Herbert Hoover's Associative State, the National Industrial Recovery Act of 1933, Technocracy, Clifford Douglas' Social Credit, and productivity-based collective bargaining, as shown in this chapter, were all attempts by government to solve the money-income prisoner's dilemma characteristic of periods of massive energy deepening.

It is my view that rather than being seen as ill-conceived policy measures—as is currently the case—all of these are consistent with the historical development and growth of market-based (read: organized) trade. The resolution of exchange-related prisoner's dilemmas, as I have tried to show, has, since time immemorial, involved governments. Without government, organized markets would not exist, money would not exist. In short, organized trade would not exist.

Further, not only is government a necessary condition for the existence of markets, it is a necessary condition for the growth of markets (income) in periods of technological change. Individual agents are, by the nature of their problem, unable to "make" markets, making cooperation the dominant strategy.

4

Nonenergy-Based Underincome

4.1 Introduction

Despite their historical importance, energy shocks are not, strictly speaking, the only possible cause of underincome. As underincome is defined as a disequilibrium between the overall level of working capital and the value of productive capacity, it follows that anything that opens up a gap between the two could, at least theoretically, lead to underincome. For example, if all producers were simultaneously to replace their workers (i.e. animate supervisors) with control devices, then aggregate working capital, in the limit, decrease to zero, thus resulting in underincome.

This chapter examines non-energy-based underincome. Cast in terms of the energy-organization approach to production developed in Chapter 2, it follows that non-energy-based causes are, by definition, organization based. That is, changes in the way in which energy is organized. Included in the latter are innovations in second-law efficiency, and innovations in what I refer to as the "supervision technology." Changes in second-law efficiency are, for the most part, the result of technological innovation. For example, James Watt's steam engine increased greatly second-law efficiency, thus increasing the amount of work which could be extracted from a given amount of energy (coal). Changes in supervision technology refer to changes in the "overseeing" of production processes. As pointed out in Beaudreau (1998), workers are, for the most part lower-level supervisors, overseeing the workings of inanimate energy-driven machines. Supervision, in turn, can be further broken down into an information component and a behavioral component, the former referring to states and the latter to behavior. For example, machine A is either working or not working, and, second, if it is not working, then the necessary remedial steps have to be taken.

In this chapter, I argue that the changes to supervision technology, made possible by the introduction of the microchip, and rendered financially viable by the energy crisis, have raised the specter of nonenergy-based underincome. By replacing workers with inanimate control technologies, the overall demand for working capital will decrease, payments to the supervisory capital now being lumped in with capital. This, in turn, will result in an imbalance between income and the value of potential output. Remember that factor payments to the supervisory input (control devices) are now residual in nature, being made once output is delivered to merchants. Specifically, it is now rolled into payments made to capital in general, which, as pointed out in Chapter 2, are a residual.

4.2 Exergy and Supervision

To understand non-energy shocks, consider Equation 3.1, reproduced here as Equation 4.1.

$$W_{ic}(t) = \eta[S_{ic}(t), T_{ic}(t)] E_{ic}(t) \qquad (4.1)$$

Here, $W_{ic}(t)$, work at time t is an increasing function of $\eta[S_{ic}(t), T_{ic}(t)]$, second-law efficiency, and $E_{ic}(t)$, energy consumption. Second law efficiency is, in turn, a function of $S_{ic}(t)$, supervision, and $T_{ic}(t)$.

Changes to supervision and tools, it then follows, qualify as non-energy shocks. For example, better tools will increase second-law efficiency, which, in turn, will increase α, the marginal revenue product of working capital (ω_{ic}). For every dollar of working capital, there will be more output, and hence, more revenue. The formal analysis of tools, defined generally, and second-law efficiency in particular, is referred to as exergy analysis. Another example is the current information and communication technology (ICT) revolution that has revolutionized supervision (control technologies) in industry. Inanimate control devices have, as a result, replaced human beings as the relevant supervisory technology. Like better tools, this has led to a manifold increase in α, the marginal revenue per dollar of working capital. The few workers (human beings) left in SMART manufacturing plants are now infinitely more productive, the latter being defined in the conventional way (i.e. output divided by labor input). I now examine each of these changes in detail.

4.2.1 Exergy Analysis

Contrary to popular belief, James Watt did not invent the steam engine. That honor goes to Denis Papin, Thomas Savary and Newcommen. Watt's claim to immortality, as it turns out, can best be understood in terms of exergy analysis, or, put differently, the analysis of maximum work potential. Watt, by introducing a separate condensing chamber to the Savary/Newcommen engine, increased efficiency from roughly 5 percent to 20 percent, making steam power commercially viable. One could argue that Watt's steam engine was an example of a non-energy based technology shock. More work could be "extracted" from a given amount of fuel, in this case, coal. Formally, this corresponded to an increase in η, second-law efficiency.

The energy crisis in the 1970s prompted renewed interest in "availability" and "work potential." As Jorgenson (1983) pointed out, real energy prices decreased monotonically throughout much of the 20th century, with the result that energy consumption mushroomed. The data on electric power consumption in U.S. manufacturing presented in the previous chapter bear this out. Energy efficiency, as pointed out in Beaudreau (1998), decreased throughout much of this period. The energy crisis, however, put an end to this. Producers, especially those in energy-intensive industries, sought out ways to increase "work availability."

The U.S. pulp and paper industry is a case in point. In his introductory remarks to a TAPPI (Technical Association of the Pulp and Paper Industry) volume devoted to "Energy Engineering and Management in the Pulp and Paper Industry," editor Matthew J. Coleman explains:

> The basic resources needed to make paper are wood, water and energy. While fiber sources can change, it is not practical to make paper without water and energy. Electricity, coal, and fuel oil are the primary purchased sources of energy, with bark and hog fuel the primary indigenous sources of fuel available to mills. Whether a mill purchases all its power, or is able to generate its own using waste for fuel, the large amounts of energy used in the pulping and paper making process have maintained the need for efficient energy management.
>
> In North America during the past decade, the pulp and paper industry has made great strides toward energy independence. The availability of waste and bark for boiler fuel has focused the strategies of fully-integrated mills into more efficient use of these energy resources, while for non-integrated mills and many European mills, the management emphasis has been on better energy efficiency and conservation.
>
> Mills which practice the best methods of energy recovery and management will benefit the most from the current instabilities in the world oil markets. The current price rise of oil is a reminder of how delicate the balance is between production and consumption of that particular fuel. Price increases in fuel oil can trigger increases in electrical power cost, and increase the substitution value of fuels such as coal, bark, and waste wood. (Coleman 1991, *i*)

Further evidence that the energy crisis has led to a fundamental shift from energy deepening to energy efficiency in the pulp and paper industry is provided by Heikko Mannisto, vice president of EKONO Inc., in Bellevue Washington, who described how energy price increases have "drastically" changed mill design in the pulp and paper industry.

> Because of the energy crisis in the early 1970's, energy conservation became one of the key issues in the North American pulp and paper industry, and most companies initiated mill wide studies on how to reduce energy consumption. Because the mills had been designed and built for low energy costs, there were suddenly more conservation measures that had a high or reasonable payback than many companies could manage. (Mannisto 1991, 21)

As this example makes clear, the emphasis today is on maximizing efficiency (η), as opposed to maximizing energy throughput (i.e. $E(t)$). Theoretically speaking, this involves bringing actual levels of energy used in production processes closer to their theoretical minimums. More energy-intensive production processes (i.e. higher throughput) no longer appear to be an option, in spite of lower energy prices owing in large measure to the pervading uncertainty over energy prices. That real energy prices have fallen over the past decade is immaterial. The emphasis is, and no doubt will continue to be, on increasing energy efficiency. The fallout, as far as the problem of underincome is concerned, can be understood in terms of α, specifically, an increase in α, leading to a decrease in ω_{ic}, producer working capital. For example, in the pulp and paper industry, existing levels of value added will require less energy, and, hence, less operating capital (ω).

4.2.2 The Information and Communications Technology Revolution

For all that has been said, and written in the popular press about the information revolution and the information age, surprisingly little is known of its causes and, more importantly, of its consequences. At a time when growth rates have plummeted, when productivity has been flat, when per-capita income, the chief measure of economic well-being, has been relatively stable, the present information and communications technology (ICT) revolution has become the proverbial knight in shining armor. Will it save the day? Will more information increase productivity, per-capita income growth, and overall economic well-being, restoring growth rates to their pre-energy crisis levels? Can we once again hope that the next generation will be better off than ours? Surprisingly, answers to these questions have been slow in coming. By answers, it should be understood, scientifically-proven predictions. Let me begin with the economics literature. As I have argued previously (Beaudreau 1998,1999a), the economics literature has surprisingly little to say about information, and, more specifically, the role of information in production processes. This stems, in large measure, from the very way in which political economists, from Adam Smith to Paul Romer, have modeled—and continue to model—production. Specifically, output (value added, transformation) is defined as an increasing function of capital and labor, with technology entering parametrically. Put starkly, technology is the production theory's theoretical portmanteau. Anything and everything is thrown into the technology variable.

This explains the present situation in which production theory, bells and whistles aside, has evolved little from the time of Adam Smith. This, however, is not to say that evolution is—or should be—an end in and of itself. The problem is that while production processes have evolved and continue to evolve, production theory has not. As pointed out in Beaudreau (1998,1999a), production processes underwent radical changes as the result of the substitution of animate, muscular energy for inanimate, fossil fuel-based energy. Brawn no longer powered production processes (transformation); instead, "fire power" was the main driving force.

Labor, up until then the primary source of energy in manufacturing (cottage industry, putting-out system), was transformed into "machine operatives," overseeing the workings of steam-powered machines. Put differently, labor was "divested" of its role as energy source, only to continue on as a supervisor, the implication being that in the putting-out system, labor oversaw the workings of looms, spinning wheels, etcetera.

Unfortunately, today mainstream production theory has, two centuries later, yet to incorporate this change, with the result that contemporary production theory is, at best, suited to the study of what are, in essence, Paleolithic production processes. That is, production processes based solely on capital (tools) and labor. The result is a theory of production devoid of both energy and organization, the latter including information.

The productivity and growth slowdown has, since, brought the issue to a head. Clearly, existing models of growth and innovation were inadequate, if only because they failed to shed light on what at the time was—and still is—a crisis. Neoclassical growth theory, Solow-Swan style, was turned on its head. Models of exogenous technology shocks, tolerable in periods of high growth (virtually all of this century), no longer cut it. Technology would have to be endogenized. The result was the vast, voluminous literature known as "endogenous growth" (Romer 1986; Aghion and Howitt 1998).

In the centuries-long tradition of classical and neoclassical economics, endogenous growth models distinguish traditional from nontraditional factor inputs, capital and labor being examples of the former, and energy and information being examples of the latter. A case in point is the burgeoning General Purpose Technology (GPT) literature, popularized by Timothy Bresnahan, Manuel Tratjenberg, and Elhanan Helpman.

> In any given "era" there typically exist a handful of technologies that play a far-reaching role in fostering technical change in a wide range of user sectors, thereby bringing about sustained and pervasive productivity gains. The steam engine during the first industrial revolution, electricity in the early part of this century and microelectronics in the pas two decades are widely thought to have played such a role. (Helpman and Tratjenberg 1994, 1)

Unfortunately, substantively speaking, this literature differs little from the early literature on growth accounting, popularized by Edward Denison. Capital and labor remain the primary factor inputs, general purpose technologies being parametric variables. Anything and everything qualifies.

As a result, there is a pressing need for a theory of production, endogenous growth theory being little more than more sophisticated bells and whistles—in short, metaphysics. While the hypotheses are many, the proofs are few. The very fact that information is lumped into the same category as the steam engine and electric power is evidence of the metaphysical nature of endogenous growth theory in general, and general purpose technology-based growth in particular. Clearly, what is needed is a theory of production sufficiently general to incorporate, in a meaningful way, tools, labor, energy and information.

4.2.3 The ICT Revolution Reexamined

In the current literature on innovation and research and development, the information revolution is often cited as a general purpose technology (GPT) (Bresnahan and Tratjenberg 1992). Other GPT's include the steam engine and electric power. This raises the obvious question, are they related, and if so, how?

The energy-organization model of production referred to earlier (Beaudreau 1998) makes an important distinction between physically-productive and organizationally-productive factor inputs. Energy is physically productive; supervision, however, is not. Like tools, it contributes to defining the production process (entropic process), as well as the corresponding level of second-law efficiency. Better supervision, it therefore follows, increases η, the level of second-law efficiency, thus allowing for more output per unit energy input (due, say, to less breakdown). It therefore follows that output is not necessarily increasing in information. In fact, one could argue that owing to congestion, more of the same information may, in fact, reduce productivity.

How then should the current information and communications technology revolution be understood? To begin with, it is imperative that the information and its role in production be understood, independent of any applications. Then, and only then, can its effects on production, productivity, etcetera, be examined.

To begin with, I would like to argue that the current information and communications technology revolution, like the first and second industrial revolutions, is energy related. Specifically, the advent of the microchip, and consequently, the personal computer (PC), increased the speed at which information (bits of information) could be transferred. Take, for example, the case of machine supervision. Computer-controlled control devices increased the amount and speed of machine-related information, relative to human being-based supervision technologies. Put differently, supervision machines consume less energy, per unit of supervision, than people-based supervision. Consequently, information can now be transferred more quickly, and, at a lower cost.

This has prompted related innovations in the area of information storage. For example, with increased CPU processing speeds (measured in MHz) has come increased information storage capacity, typically in the form of hard disk drives, capable of storing billions of bytes of information. Table 4.1 presents the various CPUs and their corresponding speeds, measured in MHz's from 1979 to 1996. We see that the 8088 CPU had a speed of 4.77 MHz, which is dwarfed by the 1996 Pentium Pro which has a speed of up to 200 MHz. The results are there for everyone to see. Owners of personal computers have access, at a low cost, to virtually unlimited amounts of information (e.g. via the internet).

Table 4.1
The PC CPU Chart

CPU Type	Year	Speed, MHz	Transitors
8088	1979	4,77	29K
80286	1982	8,10,12,20	130K
80386SX	1988	16,20,25,33	275K
80386SL	1990	16,20,25	855K
80386DX	1985	16,20,25,33	275K
80486SX	1991	16,20,25,33	900K
80486DX	1989	25,33,50	1,200K
80486DX2	1992	25/50,33/66	1,200K
80486SX	1993	25,33	1,400K
80486DX4	1994	25/75,33/100	1,600K
P5 Pentium	1994	75,90,100, 120,133,233, 450,500,800	3,300K
P6 Pentium		133,150,180, 200,400	5,500K

Source: www.a1computers.net/pcpunit.htm.

One of the major differences between the present information and communications technology revolution and the first and second industrial revolutions, however, is with regard to output. The first and second industrial revolutions, by increasing the amount of energy—and consequently, speed—consumed in manufacturing processes, increased output (e.g. textiles) per period of time. Will the information revolution do likewise? Some, like Bismal K. Bose, of the General Electric Company, who see the introduction of control systems, specifically the use of microcomputers. as the basis of "the forthcoming industrial revolution," are unequivocal.

> The advent of microcomputers since the beginning of the 1970's has brought a new dimension to power electronics and drive technology. The impact of this evolution is as significant as the advent of power semiconductor devices in the 1950's. In the forthcoming industrial revolution, that is the "computerized automation of factories," microcomputers will not only provide intelligence to higher level factory automation, but will play a vital role in the control of lower-level power electronics and motion control systems. Microcomputers have now been accepted universally for the control of power electronic and drive systems. It is interesting to note that both the ends of the power-electronics spectrum are digital: one provides the brain, and the other provides the muscle. (Bose 1987, 32)

This brings us to the key question, namely, is information productive? Will more information increase productivity, and, if so, how? To better understand the role of information in production, let us consider what engineers refer to as control technologies. Control technologies are defined as electronic and non-electronic (i.e. hydraulic) devices whose chief function consists of monitoring and supervising anthropomorphic entropic processes. The engineering literature is, as one can well imagine, replete with definitions of automation and control technologies. For example, Larry D. Jones and A. Foster Chin, in *Electronic Instruments and Measurements*, define automated or control systems in terms of information.

> Many instruments serve common purposes in supplying information about some variable quantity that is to be measured. Besides providing a visual indication of the quantity being measured, the instrument sometimes furnishes a permanent record. In addition, some instruments are used to control a quantity. Therefore, we can say that instruments serve three basic functions: indicating, recording and controlling. A particular instrument may serve all three functions simultaneously. General-purpose electrical and electronic test instruments primarily provide indicating and recording functions. The instrumentation used in industrial-process situations frequently provides a control function. The entire system may then be called a control or automated system.
>
> There are many ways to measure the value of different quantities. Some physical quantities are best measured by purely mechanical means such as using a monometer gauge to measure gas pressure. Other quantities are measured by methods that are primarily electrical such as measuring solution conductivity with a current meter. Other measurements are made with electronic instruments that contain an amplifying circuit to increase the amplitude of the quantity being measured. (Jones and Chin 1981, 2)

This allows us to draw the following inferences. First, control devices can be either animate, involving human beings, or inanimate, involving computers. Second, the information used in control devices is qualitatively, not quantitatively productive. Third, the information and communications technology revolution, as far as production processes are concerned, is more about replacing animate control devices with inanimate ones, than it is about increasing output, ceteris paribus. I begin with the second point. Information in production processes is qualitatively productive. That is, more of the same information will not increase productivity. Knowing that a machine is turning at 250 rpm's, let us presume, is a useful piece of information. Having ten employees measuring and conveying this information is not. Having better information, however, can lead to higher productivity by increasing second-law efficiency. That is, by reducing energy waste. These gains, however, are likely to be small, and, moreover, limited in scope.

If the information and communications technology revolution cannot increase productivity, defined as output per unit energy input, then how are we to understand the current interest in information? The answer, I submit, lies in the substitution of inanimate forms of supervision for animate forms. In other words, replace workers with computers, and, in the process, cut labor (supervision) costs substantially. As pointed out in Chapter 2, labor costs represent 60-65 percent of overall operating costs. Automation, it follows, is a profit-increasing (profit-doubling) strategy.

Evidence of this can be found in the trade journals where engineering consulting firms with names like "Nortek Automation" and "Wes-Tech Automation Systems" abound. Take for example, the following description of Manufacturing Cells provided by "Wes-Tech Automation Systems" on their WEB site.

> Working from a library of proven solutions, Wes-Tech is able to transform almost any manufacturing process into an unattended manufacturing cell which requires only periodic loading of raw parts or stock onto a storage and transport system. Starting with a new or existing machining center, lathe, grinder, the Wes-Tech cell concept offers a variety of parts presentation possibilities, including pallets, feeder bowls, magazines, conveyors, and work tables. Depending on your individual loading requirements, Wes-Tech can draw from a wide range of standard, modular turnings and machining center loader and accessories that meet your needs. For lower labor content and increased quality as a result of a consistent loading system, Wes-Tech's manufacturing cells are your answer to efficient, unattended machining. (www.westech.com/manufacturing.html)

4.2.4 The Energy Crisis, Exergy and the ICT Revolution

The choice of high-efficiency tools (exergy) and automated control systems (information) as the two non-energy technological shocks was not entirely fortuitous. As I have argued in Beaudreau (1998), both were responses to the energy crisis and the ensuing productivity slowdown. Higher energy prices prompted manufacturing firms the world over to (1) reduce energy consumption, (2) find new, more energy-efficient production processes (use energy more wisely (productively), and (3) accelerate the shift from animate (human) supervision technologies, to inanimate ones. The first is self-evident. The second is simply applied exergy analysis, while the third is commonly known as rationalizing or downsizing. As higher energy prices cut into profit margins, producers responded by cutting costs, specifically labor costs.[1] Advances in information and communications technology, especially in the area of industrial controls, reduced the demand for animate forms of supervision (labor), thus decreasing the demand for operating capital per unit value of output (value added).

4.2.5 ICT-Resistant Production Processes and Globalization

Not all production processes are amenable to ICT-based supervision technologies. Take, for example, the clothing industry where production processes continue to be highly labor intensive, owing, in large measure, to the high number of manual operations (e.g. jeans). As pointed out in Beaudreau (1998), in ICT-resistant industries, the energy crisis led profit-maximizing producers to shift their operations to low-wage off-shore localizations and, in the process, increase their profits. Table 4.2 presents average hourly wages for garment workers as reported by *Womens Wear Daily.*

Table 4.2
Average Hourly Wages for Garment Workers

Country	U.S. Dollars	Country	U.S. Dollars
Bangladesh	0.16	Burma	0.18
Canada	9.88	China	0.68
Columbia	1.05	Costa Rica	2.38
Dominican Republic	1.62	Eastern Europe	1.11
El Salvador	1.38	France	7.81
Germany	23.19	Guatemala	1.25
Haiti	0.49	Honduras	1.31
Hong Kong	4.55	India	0.26
Indonesia	0.34	Italy	14.00
Jamaica	1.80	Macau	2.41
Mexico	1.08	Nicaragua	0.76
Pakistan	0.21	Philippines	0.94
Sri Lanka	0.31	Thailand	1.02
United Kingdom	7.38	United States	9.56
Vietnam	0.26		

Table 4.3 presents the percentage change in employment in the textiles, clothing and footwear (TCLF) industries over the period 1980–1993. We see, for

example, that job creation occurred principally in low-wage countries, while job destruction occurred in high-wage countries.

What is important to note, as far as off-shore relocalization is concerned, is the nature of the underlying production processes, namely as being "control-technology resistant." While control technologies have eliminated lower-level supervisors in many industries, they have failed to make significant inroads in the TCLF industries. Process engineers have yet to develop completely automated clothing and footwear equipment (pneumatic or electronic). If and when they do, there is good reason to believe that these industries will be footloose, in the sense that they will no longer migrate exclusively to low-wage countries.

4.2.6 The ICT Revolution, Globalization, and The Demand for Working Capital

It goes without saying that the ICT revolution and globalization have affected producers' demand for working capital. In cases in which control devices replaced workers, the demand for labor has decreased, while in cases in which producers relocalized to low-wage, offshore localizations, the wage bill, as the classical political economists referred to it, has also decreased.

Table 4.3
Job Creation and Job Destruction in the TCLF Industries

Country	% Change	Country	% Change
Finland	-71.7	Mauritius	344.6
Sweden	-65.4	Indonesia	177.4
Norway	-64.9	Morocco	166.5
Austria	-51.5	Jordan	160.8
Poland	-51.0	Jamaica	101.7
Syria	-50.0	Malaysia	101.2
France	-45.4	Mexico	85.1
Hungary	-43.1	China	57.3
Netherlands	-41.7	Iran	34.0
United Kingdom	-41.5	Turkey	33.7
New Zealand	-40.9	Philippines	31.8
Germany	-40.2	Honduras	30.5
Spain	-35.3	Chile	27.2
Australia	-34.7	Kenya	16.1
Argentina	-32.9	Israel	13.4
United States	-30.1	Venezuela	7.9

Source: International Labour Office (1996).

Figure 4.1, taken from Beaudreau (1998), illustrates the decline in labor's factor income (value added) share from 1958 to 1993. Disaggregated into production and nonproduction workers, we see that the former have been the hardest hit, as their share of manufacturing value added has declined by roughly 80 percent. Nonproduction workers have fared better, which is not surprising. In fact, despite the new ICTs, their share has remained relatively constant. This, I maintain, owes to the fact that ICTs and nonproduction workers are complementary factor inputs in the sense that automated equipment (e.g. robots) requires highly-trained technicians and engineers.

Figure 4.1
Factor Income Shares, U.S. Manufacturing 1958–1993

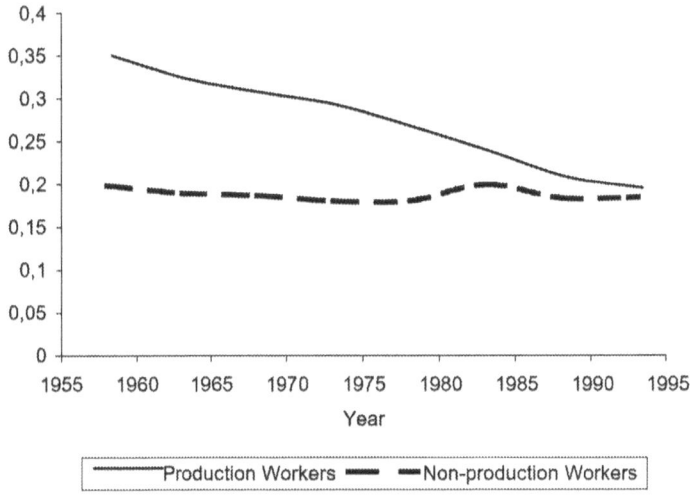

4.3 Nonenergy-Based Underincome

It stands to reason that the ICT revolution and globalization, as defined here, will have a direct impact on exchange. Specifically, by decreasing the amount of operating capital per unit value of output (value added), the substitution of animate supervision for inanimate supervision, and off-shore relocalization of labor-intensive production processes, raises the specter of underincome. While producer profits will increase in the short-run, the result of lower operating costs (and operating capital), aggregate operating capital (income) will decrease, which, in the long run, may have real effects.

Formally, the ICT revolution and globalization increase α, the productivity of ω_{ic}, producer ic operating capital. That is, each unit of operating capital (e.g. dollar, pound, franc) is more productive. To produce the same amount of value added now requires less operating capital. At the individual producer level, expected profits rise as a result according to Equation 3.4. In this case, $d\omega_{ic}$ is less than zero, which, for β/n less than one, results in an increase in profits ($d\pi_{ic}$ greater than one).

This is not the end of the story. If all $2n$ producers substitute inanimate supervision technology for animate supervision, or globalize, then ω_c, aggregate consumption good sector operating capital, and ω_k, aggregate capital good sector operating capital, will decrease, which, in turn, will lead to a decrease ω_m, merchant operating capital, the merchant anticipating a decrease in the demand for consumption goods.

Clearly, this could set off a series of events that could lead to a recession or depression. The more merchants decrease their demand for consumption and capital goods, the more producers will reduce their demand for operating capital, and so on and so forth. The important point, as far as this chapter is concerned, is that underincome can result from non-energy related shocks, in this case, changes in second-law efficiency, and the development of inanimate control technologies.

4.3.1 Instantaneous Profits

Unlike energy deepening-based underincome, where the technology shock does not lead to an increase in profits, non-energy deepening-based underincome does lead to an instantaneous increase in profits. By reducing labor costs (supervision costs), producer profits rise instantaneously.[2] Revenues are not affected; operating costs, however, decrease significantly. This stands in contrast with energy deepening-based underincome, where production capacity increases, without affecting operating costs, and, hence, overall aggregate income (operating costs).

Take, for example, the garment industry. Table 3.1 presents average hourly wages for garment workers as reported by *Womens Wear Daily*, a trade journal. We see that, converted in U.S. dollars, the average wage in Bangladesh and Burma, at $0.10–0.16, is one percent of the average wage in the United States. Thus, by relocalizing in Bangladesh or Burma, U.S. garment producers virtually eliminate labor costs, which, it goes without saying, works wonders on the bottom line. Table 3.2 presents changes in employment in the textile, clothing and footwear industries, as reported by the *International Labour Office* in Geneva (International Labor Office 1996). We see that from 1980 to 1993, jobs have been destroyed in the North (high-wage countries), and created in the South (low wage countries).

4.3.2 The Asian Contagion: Underincome at Work?

As shown in the previous chapter, pre-energy crisis profit growth was non-dialectical in nature. Energy deepening in the form of monotonically-increasing electric power consumption per production worker, increased energy rents, which, in turn, were shared by labor, capital, and, government in the form of wages, profits, and taxes. Post-energy crisis profit growth, by contrast, has been dialectical. The owners of capital, through automation and off-shore investment (globalization) have successfully increased their share of value added (income) at the expense of labor.

The incentives to move off-shore, are, as pointed out above, substantial. Producers can reduce their operating costs (chiefly labor costs), and, in the process, increase earnings. Problems arise, however, at the aggregate—in this case global—level. First, global operating capital, defined as the sum of national operating capital, decreases as a result. High-paid workers in the North are replaced by low-paid workers in the South. In the short-run, profits will rise. The problem, however, arises in the long-run. Global operating capital decreases, decreasing the merchant's demand for consumption and capital goods. Off-shore job creation comes at the expense of on-shore job-destruction. No new jobs are created. More importantly, global operating capital decreases, thus weakening the demand for consumption and capital goods.

This, I argue, is a fair characterization of the state of the world economy at the time of writing. Automation and globalization have increased short-run profits, but failed to generate the income (operating capital) growth needed to sustain (justify) the existing global capacity. As was the case in 1929, the stock market is overvalued, not vis-à-vis capacity, but rather vis-à-vis income (exchange medium). The fundamentals, by which it should be understood, productive capacity, are sound; what isn't, however, is the exchange technology.

If one combines this with a number of region-specific developments, one better understands the Asian Contagion. As producers in the North relocalized their labor-intensive production processes to the South (Asia, Central and South America), the demand for industrial infrastructure (energy, transport) increased. Host-country governments, wanting to attract off-shore investment (multinationals), responded with massive public works programs, financed, in large measure, by foreign investors. Figure 3.3 shows the cumulative development of private power capacity for four southeast Asian countries, Indonesia, Malaysia, Philippines and Thailand, from 1991 to 1997, and projections for the years 1998–2001. We see that capacity for all countries literally "took-off" in the mid-1990's, doubling, tripling, and quadrupling every few years.

Combining the lack of global income growth with massive public infrastructure investment, most of which being privately-funded, resulted in what I call market susceptibility. As Gray and Schuster (1998) point out: "Countries around the world have increasingly turned to the private sector to finance and build new power plants. This trend has been especially pronounced in Asia, which accounts for nearly 60 percent of all new private generation capacity in the developing world" (Gray and Schuster 1998, 1). Investors were betting on ever-increasing levels of foreign direct investment, and, consequently, ever-increasing levels of host-country exports to the North. What they failed to appreciate, however, was the dialectic nature of investment in the South. Foreign direct investment by multinational firms did not create any new jobs, in the aggregate, but, instead, displaced jobs from the North to the South. Global income did not increase, nor even stay the same, it decreased.

The onset of the crisis, I argue, occurred when export growth began to slow in the mid-1990s, and dropped sharply in 1996. According to Steven Radelet and Jeffrey D. Sachs:

> Fourth, export growth, measured in current U.S. dollars, began to slow in the mid-1990s and then dropped sharply in 1996 in every country. In Thailand, exports actually fell in nominal dollar terms in 1996, while in Korea, exports increased by only 3.7 percent. Several factors probably contributed to this pattern: the increasing overvaluation of the exchange rates, the appreciation of the Japanese yen against the dollar after 1994, the devaluation of the Chinese yuan in January 1994, the competitive effects of Mexico's participation in NAFTA and the devaluation of the Mexican peso, and the worldwide glut in semiconductor production. (Radelet and Sachs 1998, 24)

It is important to point out that it was not the many multinational firms present in Asia that provoked the crisis, but rather investors, betting on continuing—and even increasing—relocalization. Put differently, unlike Indonesia, Malaysia, the Philippines, and Thailand which invested heavily in public infrastructure without any assurances that the services in question (e.g. electric power) would find a market (producers), multinational firms invested knowing that there would be a market for their output, namely existing markets. When Mattel produces "Barbies" in China, it knows exactly when and where they will be sold (i.e. in their existing marketing network).

4.4 The ICT Revolution, Globalization, and "Making the Market"

It is perhaps worthwhile to reiterate the main findings of this chapter. First, the ICT revolution and globalization, both prompted by the energy crisis, have reduced the demand for working capital at the individual producer level, thus decreasing aggregate world working capital. While increasing short-run profits, it has decreased aggregate producer working capital, and, consequently, has weakened markets. In short, the global market is one big prisoner's dilemma. Each producer is trying to reduce costs—increase profits—by adopting new ICTs, and/or relocalizing production facilities offshore.

This raises what I believe to be the most fundamental question as far as the problem of underincome is concerned, namely, in the future, who will make the market? Prior to industrialization, governments made the market, financing their expenditure from taxation. During industrialization, producers collectively made the market by purchasing labor using their working capital. In what some are calling the post-industrial era, who will make the market? In a world in which ICTs make conventional workers redundant, in which all income is residual in nature, and in which government is excluded, who will make the market?

4.5 Henry Ford and Robert Eaton: A Study in Contrasts

Wage policy in the 20th century at the Ford Motor Company of Detroit, Michigan provides us with a stark example of the cost exacted by "exchange technology ignorance." Throughout his tenure as chief executive officer of the Ford Motor Company, a company he founded in 1903, Henry Ford made higher wages (nominal and real) a cornerstone of company policy. Starting with the five-dollar day in 1914, which doubled wage rates, Henry Ford raised wages at the Ford Motor Company throughout the 1910's, 1920's and 1930's, making the market in the process. This stands in stark contrast with Robert Eaton, CEO of Ford in the 1980's and 1990's, who, like his industry rivals, has decreased labor costs by outsourcing and off-shore production, hence unmaking the market. According to a piece entitled "Chrysler, Ford edge GM in cost, report says," The Detroit News reported:

> Chrysler Corp. and Ford Motor Co. enjoy substantial cost savings over General Motors Corp. by relying on outside suppliers to build many parts and components. Chrysler spends $2,167 on all labor costs per vehicle for all components, compared to $2,322 at Ford Motor Co., and $2,765 at GM, Harbour and Associates Inc. of Troy said in a report released Monday. The UAW is pressing Chrysler and Ford to build more parts and employ more workers as part of national labor talks this summer. The union also hopes to preserve the 177,000 U.S. and Canadian parts-making jobs at GM. Chrysler has 41,00 parts employees; Ford has 75,000. (*The Detroit News*, June 25, 1996, 3).

Both forms of behavior, I argue, affect underincome. In the case of Ford, the five-dollar, the six-dollar and the seven-dollar day were attempts on his part at single-handedly solving the problem of underincome in the U.S. economy in the 1910's, 1920's and 1930's. In the case of Eaton, outsourcing and off-shore production have contributed and continue to contribute to the problem of underincome in the 1990's.

Despite his carefully-crafted, folksy image, Henry Ford, a man with little formal training (see Nye 1983), understood the workings of exchange and markets. In fact, I would venture to say that he had an understanding of the model of markets and exchange presented in Chapter 1. He understood the role of producers in generating income (making the market). He understood the role of merchants in making the market, perhaps owing to the fact that he set up a network of automobile dealers. Consider the following excerpt from *The New York Times*, in which he refers to the problem of underincome:

> We've got to stop that gouging process if we want to see all of the people reasonably prosperous. There is only one rule for industrialists and that is: Make the best quality of goods possible at the lowest cost paying the highest wages possible. Nothing can be right in this country until wages are right. The life of business comes forth from the people in orders. The factories are not stopped for lack of money but for lack of orders. Money loaned at the top means nothing. Money spent at the bottom starts everything. I think that if industrial leaders had been willing to push wages up and up during the last thirty years the present economic ills would at least not be as great as they are. If the government can help in these matters, well and good, but the government has not a rosy record in running itself thus far. (*New York Times*, June 16, 1933, 4)

Throughout his career, Ford increased wage income at the Ford Motor Company, believing that if others did likewise, wages, profits, growth, and overall economic well being would increase. At the height of the Great Depression, Ford, oblivious to the intricacies of the prisoner's dilemma (Nash game in wage income), pleaded with his fellow businessmen to increase wages and decrease prices. Needless to say, few were those who heeded his advice. Today, the company he founded is engaged in measures which, while profitable in the short run, will ultimately weaken the global economy. Job destruction in the North and job creation in the South contributes to the problem of underincome, and, in the process, increases the probability of a crisis.

4.6 Conclusions

As I have attempted to demonstrate in this chapter, the problem of underincome is not technology-shock specific. While energy deepening has, over the past two centuries, been the principal cause, it is by no means the only one. Information and communications technology-related innovations, by decreasing the demand for operating capital, can result in underincome. Moreover, the results of this chapter serve to highlight the fact that the problem of underincome is an exchange-related problem, having little to do with production technology per se. Private incentives are such that overall income is less than the value of overall output. No one producer or merchant can resolve the underlying coordination failure. I now turn and examine the implications of underincome for the stock market, specifically, stock market prices.

5

Underincome and the Stock Market

The stock market rose after the war above the pre-war level by 50-100 per-
cent because of war inflation, and that since, it has doubled because of
increasing prosperity from less stable money, new mergers, new scientific
management, and the new labor policy of waste saving.

—Irving Fisher, *New York Times*, October 24, 1929

5.1 Introduction

As the word itself implies, underincome is about untapped potential, about
resources not being used fully, and consequently, about the economy producing
below its capacity. Potential output, measured by maximum throughput capacity, exceeds actual output and income. At the producer level, rated plant throughput exceeds actual plant output. At the aggregate level, aggregate throughput
exceeds aggregate output. The presence of underincome, however, raises a number of subsidiary, yet important questions. First in terms of importance is the
question of overall awareness or knowledge. For example, who in society would
know that rated plant throughput, whether at the individual producer level or the
aggregate economy-wide level, exceeds, by a considerable amount, actual plant
output? While individual process engineers would know, who else would? Would
investors? Second, assuming that some subset of the general population does in
fact know, would the information in question have real effects. That is, how
would it affect their behavior. For example, would share prices be bid up as a consequence?

This chapter focuses on the relationship between underincome and the stock
market, with particular emphasis on U.S. stock market prices in the 20th century. Using the analytical framework developed in Chapter 2, I argue that the

large persistent deviations from the efficient markets model of U.S. stock prices in the twentieth century (Shiller 1981,1989) can be explained, in large measure, by the joint occurrence of energy-deepening-based and organization-based underincome, and government policy. Put differently, overcapacity (underincome) is not a sufficient condition for share prices to rise. Also present must be some policy measure or measures aimed at resolving the underlying coordination failure.

In the mid-to-late 1920's, rational, fully-informed forward-looking investors, buoyed by the proposed higher tariffs on imported manufactures Smoot-Hawley tariff bill of 1929) aimed at closing the gap between potential and actual output, bid stock prices up, the result of which was the stock market boom. From January 1928 to September 1929, stock prices increased 100 percent. In the post-WWII period, further energy deepening, in the form of what Alfred Chandler referred to as the "intensified application of energy," prompted further deviations from the efficient markets model.

The chapter is organized as follows. I begin with a brief review of the literature on market volatility, specifically Robert Shiller's extensive work on excess volatility. This is then followed by a model of underincome-based excess market volatility, of which there are two types, namely energy-deepening based and organization based. Lastly, I present some evidence.

5.2 Stock Market Volatility

The literature on market volatility has, until recently, been sparse, dominated, in large measure by the work of Robert J. Shiller of Yale University, who has spent the past two decades studying the U.S. stock market (Shiller 1981,1989). The upshot of his work is relatively straightforward, namely that, regardless of how expected dividends are modeled, "measures of stock price volatility over the past century appear to be far too high—five to thirteen times too high—to be attributed to new information about real dividends (Shiller 1981, 434). Theoretically, the variance (standard deviation) of the forecasted share price and the variance (standard deviation) of the forecasting error should be equal to the variance (standard deviation) of the actual share price. This follows directly from the fact that the covariance between the forecasted share price and the forecasting error is, by definition, zero. Otherwise, as Shiller points out, forecasts could be improved (i.e. are not optimal).

Figures 5.1 and 5.2 are taken from his 1981 *American Economic Review paper*, which led to his 1989 book entitled *Market Volatility*. Notwithstanding what appears to be white noise around the trend, we can identify three periods of excess optimism, and three periods of excess pessimism—that is with regard to dividends. The former include the period from the turn of the century to 1914, the period from 1926 to 1929, and the period from 1955 to 1970. The latter include the period from 1914 to 1925, the period from 1929 to 1932, and the period from 1945 to 1955.

Unfortunately, little is known about these period of excess optimism and excess pessimism. Large upward swings in stock prices are viewed as speculative bubbles, the stock market boom of 1926 to 1929 being the most celebrated. Joseph Stiglitz defined the intuition underlying speculative bubbles as "if the reason that the price is high today is only because investors believe that the selling price will be high tomorrow—when "fundamental" factors do not seem to justify such a price—then a bubble exists (Stiglitz 1990, 13). Regarding the stock market boom and crash of the late 1920's, stock market speculation, combined with un-savvy monetary policy on the part of the Federal Reserve—intended to help Great Britain reestablish the $4.86 pound—led to the boom in prices. In time, the bubble popped, and, in the process, provided a consistent rationalization for the ensuing periods of excess pessimism (White 1990).

While this view predominates in the literature, it suffers from a number of shortcomings, not the least of which is the lack of microfoundations. How do bubbles arise? What are the instigating factors? How do they assume a life of their own? Are they purely spontaneous?

Figure 5.1
Real Standard and Poor's Composite Stock Price Index, 1871–1979

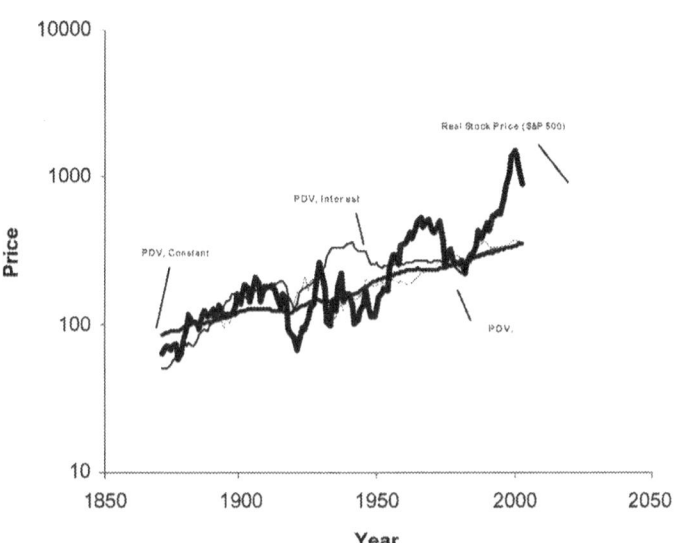

While this view predominates in the literature, it suffers from a number of In *Market Volatility*, published in 1989, Robert Shiller begins to address these issues, breaking down the traditional barriers between economics and psychology and sociology. Social psychology- and sociology-based models are presented. Social movements, fashions and fads are offered as contributing factors, and evidence is presented. He concludes that:

> The most important reason for expecting that stock prices are heavily influenced by social dynamics comes from the observation of participants in the market and of human nature as presented in the literature on social psychology, sociology, and marketing. A study of the history of the U.S. stock market in the postwar period suggests that various social movements were under way in this period that might plausibly have major effects on the aggregate demand for shares. Must we rely on such evidence to make the case against market efficiency? Yes; there is no alternative to human judgment in understanding human behavior. (Shiller 1989, 41)

Absent from Shiller's list of possible causes, however, is non-market clearing (i.e. non-Walrasian) phenomena. For example, what if productive capacity increases (jumps), but, for any number of reasons, actual output fails to increase, in the short and medium run? Further, what if the government were to institute policies (macro, trade) aimed at closing the gap, the efficacy of which was unknown? How would this affect stock prices? In this case, it is perfectly reasonable to expect that stock prices would have little bearing on current dividends.

Such reasoning is what Shiller sees as constituting a popular model. Specifically, investors, aware of the presence of a technological shock, are buoyed by new policy measures aimed at closing the gap between potential and actual output, the result of which is higher share prices. However, whereas he describes such models as being "usually simple, unsophisticated, and spontaneous," this model is, at least potentially, more sophisticated than the efficient-markets model in its view of the workings of a market economy.

In the remainder of this chapter, I shall attempt to show how, by adopting an alternative model of production (energy and organization), and by introducing underincome, the excess volatility of U.S. stock prices reported by Robert Shiller (1981,1989) can be rationally explained. More precisely, stock price optimism results from the joint presence of changing fundamentals (electric power-based energy deepening) and third-party intervention (government policy). Stock price pessimism, in general, results from the failure of the latter to resolve the underlying coordination failure, the crash of 1929 being the most celebrated case in point. I end by discussing the excess volatility in the 1990's.

5.3 Analytical Framework

The two-sector, disaggregated producer-merchant model of economic activity presented in Chapter 2 is used here to study the link between the joint presence of technological change and underincome, on one hand, and unexplained stock market volatility on the other. By now, it should be clear that underincome implies the existence of a gap between potential output and actual output, the latter being equal to actual income. In Chapters 3 and 4, energy and non-energy causes of underincome were studied. Steam power in the nineteenth century and electric power in the twentieth century were cited as examples of energy-based underincome. On the other hand, automation was cited as an example of non-energy-based underincome.

Common to both forms of underincome is a marked increase in α, the average and marginal productivity of operating capital (primarily labor costs). Energy deepening, by increasing the throughput rate, reduces the labor cost (lower-level supervision costs) per unit of output. Automation does likewise by reducing ω_{ic}

for a given level of V_{ic}, value added. Equation 5.1 models both effects. An increase in e_{ic} increases α, as does an increase in o_{ic}, the organization metric.

$$\alpha = \alpha[e_{ic}, o_{ic}] \qquad (5.1)$$

5.3.1 Capacity, Policy and Expected Profits

As argued in Beaudreau (1998,1999), the rise of material civilization over the course of the past two hundred years parallels the course of energy-deepening in industry, the process whereby more and more energy is consumed per per of time, and per capita, resulting in greater and greater wealth.[1] The Watt-Boulton rotary steam engine, the Trevithick-Woolf high-pressure steam engine, the Parsons steam turbine, and the electro-magnetic motor in its various forms (DC, AC, inductive, high speed) all increased vastly the productivity—and hence, rated capacity—of existing production processes. This raises a key question, namely how did the market for the property rights over production processes (the organization of energy), better known as the stock market (industrials) react to these innovations? Did the news of impending productivity increases serve to bid prices up?

This serves to raise an important theoretical question, namely what is the relationship between energy deepening-based productivity shocks and stock market prices? Related issues include, but are not limited to, questions such as, are investors informed of these shocks, and, if so, how? Is knowledge of energy-based productivity shocks a sufficient condition for bidding stock prices up?

Let us begin with the first, are investors informed of energy deepening-based shocks, and, if so how? The answer to this question is, by no means, obvious, owing, in large measure, to the nebulous, intangible nature of information. Information used by investors and investment firms is not published, at least not in general.

Consider the electrification of U.S. industry referred to in Chapter 3. Were investors aware of the profit opportunities the shift from water and steam-based belting, gearing and shafting drive to electric drive offered? The available information is somewhat sketchy. David Nye, in *Electrifying America*, suggests that businessmen, like engineers, were aware of potential, specifically the potential for profit, electrification offered.

> Businessmen regarded electrification differently than did the general public, the intellectuals, or the emerging technical elite. As readers of Century, Suc-

cess, Magazine of Wall Street, World's Work, and similar publications, they saw it not as a potentially dangerous form of social power, nor as a utopian technology, nor as a mysterious new power in medicine, nor as a tool for rationalizing society; rather, they embraced electrification as an instrument for making profits. (Nye 1990, 168)

This would suggest that electrification per se was a sufficient condition for stock prices to rise. That is, acting on information of a τ percent increase in productivity/capacity, investors would bid stock prices up by some multiple of τ. Unfortunately, such a view ignores the problems referred to in this book, specifically, the problem of underincome.[2] The mere presence of capacity, as I have shown, is not a sufficient condition for output, supply and demand. Rated capacity can increase throughout the economy without there being a concomitant increase income, supply and demand.

A related question is one of magnitude. If rated plant capacity increases by τ percent, ceteris paribus, then by how much will expected profits and dividends increase? For example, will they increase by τ percent, or will they increase by more, or less? Clearly, the answer to this question depends largely on investors' wage expectations. That is, how investors see wages evolving in relationship to potential productivity. Put differently, how do investors see the technology shock affecting expected real wages? If investors' expect them to rise by τ percent, then it stands to reason that expected profit and dividend growth would also rise by τ percent. On the other hand, if they expect wages to remain constant—owing to the presence of excess supply in the labor market—then, it stands to reason that expected profits would rise by more than τ. Formally, in this case, expected profits would rise by τ divided by capital's share of value added. For example, if τ is 0.40 and capital's share of value added is 0.30, then expected profits will rise by 133 percent.

This raises another important question, namely, were (are) investors aware of the problem of underincome? Is news of a new, capacity-increasing technological change (electrification) sufficient for a commensurate increase in earning expectations? Just how do investors respond?

Analytically speaking, the problem is the data. As with all forms and types of expectations, data do not exist. This, however, serves to raise a number of related questions, namely, is the representative investor aware of possible income-related coordination failures, and other "making the market"-related problems?

Not surprisingly, little research has been done on such issues. As pointed out earlier, issues relating to the making of markets have been, in general, ignored in economics, with the result that today, little is known. Consequently, given the paucity of theoretical and empirical work, it is more than likely that the representative investor would be unaware of underincome, and its implications. After all, underincome is a social (read: group) phenomenon.

This raises another question, namely, would those individuals representing investors in general, or producers in general, be aware? After all, it stands to reason that, given their constituency, they would be particularly interested in aggregates (aggregate share prices, aggregate profits, aggregate sales, etcetera). There is some evidence, albeit scant, that chambers of commerce have been, at various points in time, been aware of the problem of making the market. Take, for example, the case of Henry I. Harriman, president of the U.S. Chamber of Commerce, who, on the day the National Industrial Recovery Act (NIRA) became law, declared:

> Today's passage of the NIRA constitutes a most important step in our progress towards business rehabilitation. It should begin immediately to bring about a large measure of reemployment and an increase in buying power throughout the country. The act itself will permit legitimate business enterprise to lift itself above the destructive competition which has prevented recovery and which has been threatening to bring about complete economic demoralization. With reasonable opportunity to work together, business enterprise might earlier have mitigated the effects of the depression. Continued denial of that opportunity, with a consequently great amount of business wreckage, would inevitably have renewed an era of mergers and combinations that followed earlier depressions and would have given rise to problems which the country, in the public interest, should be spared. This act now permits through voluntary agreements public benefits heretofore denied. The act will permit American producers, determined to protect American standards of living, from being forced through cut-throat competition to lower standards. An immediate and widespread participation by industry and commerce in the benefits supplied by the act will quickly put large numbers of men to work and will immediately act to spur business generally. (*New York Times*, June 14, 1933, 2)

Harriman, it should be noted, was the exception. Few industrial and financial leaders were aware of the problem at hand, let alone the means by which to resolve it. To this very day, underincome in particular, and coordination failures in general are, for the most part, ignored in the teaching of basic economics.

5.3.2 Investors and Productivity Growth

In this section, I shall argue that while investors are, in general, not aware of the problem of underincome per se, they are, and have been, aware of the intricacies of productivity shocks-based value growth, namely the joint presence of a technology shock, and some form of coordination device. I shall focus on two periods of what I refer to as excessive stock price optimism, the stock market boom and crash of 1929, and the current stock market boom. Underlying each is a technological shock-based increase in anticipated earnings. The stock market boom and crash of 1929, as I argued in Beaudreau (1996a), was based largely on two factors, namely the electrification of U.S. industry and the proposed changes to America's tariff laws contained in the Republican electoral platform in the 1928 presidential elections. Throughout much of the 1920's, excess capacity had been building throughout most sectors of the U.S. economy. Rated plant capacity skyrocketed with the introduction of electric drive. The stock market, however, did not, for the most part, factor these increases in stock prices. The latter remained relatively constant in the early 1920's, a time when rated output (potential output) was soaring.

The reason is relatively simple. Rated capacity, in the minds of investors, is not a sufficient condition for actual capacity. That all production processes in America could produce 30 percent more was of no consequence to actual production, income, expenditure, and, most importantly, profits.

As it turned out, it was not until the government entered the fray that investors perked up, so to speak. Rumblings about higher tariffs, prohibitive tariffs aimed at keeping out imports, and, consequently, making room for more domestic goods, set stock prices onto an upward spiral. The reason was straightforward, namely that tariffs would, via import substitution, "make the markets" necessary for the increased—if not full—utilization of the new rated plant capacity. Put differently, the stock market boom of 1928–1929 can be advanced as evidence that investors were aware of the problem of underincome.

More evidence comes from the recent stock market boom, based on organization-based changes in the workplace, specifically, automation and off-shore production. Automation and off-shore production, by reducing α, have increased expected earnings and profits. In the limiting case of α going to zero (no working capital), expected profits increase by 233 percent.

Clearly, such behavior is unsustainable as a Nash equilibrium. The point however, is that investors have been, and continue to be, aware of the income dimension. Stock prices are bid up on the assumption—false as it may be—that the producer's sales (overall income) will not be affected by its actions.

5.3.3 Estimating Technology Shocks Using Stock-Market Data

As argued in Beaudreau (1996a), the stock market boom of 1928–1929 was the direct result of the Hoover administrations tariff initiative. By further restricting foreign producers access to the U.S. market, the tariff hikes proposed in the Smoot-Hawley Tariff Bill would provide U.S. producers with a larger share of the domestic market. Sales, earnings, and profits, it was anticipated, would increase as a result. Investors reacted by bidding up the price of shares. According to basic financial analysis, the greater the anticipated increase in earnings, the greater the price increase. Ceteris paribus, if investors expected earnings to rise by τ percent, then stock prices should increase by an equivalent amount.

This forms the basis of the estimates of τ, the technology shock, reported in this section. Specifically, I infer values for τ from stock-price movements in the period under consideration. I begin by examining in detail the relationship between a technology shock and expected earnings/dividends. Basic theory predicts that if the underlying technological change is of the Hicks-neutral variety, then both labor and capital productivity should increase commensurately, as both are more productive. Wages and dividends ought to increase accordingly. However, as shown in Chapter 2, there are no private incentives for producers to increase wages. This raises an important question, namely how do investors in general, and investors in the 1920s in particular, see the relationship between technological change and real wages. For example, when estimating the earnings potential of the introduction of a new technology, do they factor in wage increases? Analytically, this amounts to asking whether investors play a Nash strategy as opposed to a rational strategy vis-à-vis wages. In other words, do they take the wage as given (i.e., the Nash strategy), or do they factor wage increases into expected earnings (i.e., the rational strategy)?

Admittedly, this is an empirical question. For investors to factor wage increases into stock prices, it would have to be the case that historically, process innovations systematically led to real wage hikes; otherwise, there would be little reason to believe that investors would do so. On this note, the theoretical and empirical evidence indicates the absence of any one-to-one relationship between real wages and productivity. As was shown in Chapter 2, producers have no private incentives to increase real wages. Moreover, the data show nominal and real wages in U.S. manufacturing to be constant throughout this period in spite of important productivity increases. It would therefore not be unreasonable to conclude that investors in the late 1920s adopted what amounted to a Nash strategy vis-à-vis wages. This has important implications for the behavior of expected dividends and, hence, stock prices. For example, it implies that since the proportion of earnings-to-capital constitutes a fraction (i.e., roughly 30 percent) of total producer income, expected dividends would increase by more than τ percent. Specifically, they would increase by a multiple of τ. Consider the following numerical example. Let δ define the ratio of capital income to total producer income. Suppose that $\delta = 0.3$. Hypothetical total producer income of $100 would yield factor payments to capital on the order of $30, which, capitalized at a rate of interest of 3 percent per annum, would yield a stock value of $1,000. Now, assume that τ takes on a value of 0.40. That is, the process innovation in question increases productivity by 40 percent. For a constant nominal wage, the resulting share value would rise to $2,333, as the anticipated $40 rise in earnings would be factored totally into share prices. The rate at which the hypothetical share price would rise is given as τ/δ, which in this case corresponds to 1.33 (133 percent). Thus, what would in normal circumstances, be a 40 percent increase in share value is magnified by a factor of 3.325. I applied this simple technique to estimate τ_s, τ_m τ_r, and τ_u the implicit-in-share price technology shock in the economy as a whole, manufacturing (industrials), railroads and utilities, respectively, using the corresponding Standard and Poor's indexes of stock market prices from 1923 to 1929. Referring to Table 5.1, we see that total, industrial, railroad, and utilities real share prices increased some 238, 231, 102, and 230 percent, respectively, from 1924 to 1929. This implies that by 1929, initial hypothetical book value of $1,000 in each of these sectors would have risen to $3,380 for the market as a whole, $3,310 for manufacturing, $2,020 for railroads, and $3300 for utilities. For these to exist as financial market equilibria, anticipated sector earnings of $101.40, $99.30, $60.60 and $99.00 are required, which, when initial earnings of 30.00are netted out, yield values for τ_s, τ_m τ_r, and τ_u of 71, 69, 31, and 69 percent, respectively.

The way to interpret these results is as follows. Hypothetical fully-informed investors, knowing that τ_s, τ_m τ_r, and τ_u stood at 71, 69, 31 and 69 percent (respectively) would have bid up the value of market, industrial, railroad, and utility shares by 238, 231, 102, and 230 percent (respectively). In other words, changing fundamentals in the presence of relatively constant real wages would have led investors to bid share prices up by 238, 231, 102 and 230 percent respectively. What is interesting to note is the fact that the greatest gains occurred in those sectors of the U.S. economy most likely to be affected by electrification, notably industry and, of course, utilities.

Table 5.1
Stock Market-Based Estimates of τ

1924–1929

Stock Index	Value 1929	Value 1923	Growth	τ
Total (S&P)	56.42	16.71	238	0.71
Industrials (S&P)	42.19	12.74	231	0.69
Industrials (DJIA)	352.51	95.52	269	0.81
Railroads (S&P)	91.27	45.13	102	0.31
Utilities (S&P)	117.25	35.30	230	0.69

1925-1929

Stock Index	Value 1929	Value 1924	Growth	τ
Total (S&P)	51.42	17.67	191	57
Industrials (S&P)	42.19	13.34	216	65
Industrials (DJIA)	352.51	120.51	192	57
Railroads (S&P)	91.27	48.86	87	26
Utilities (S&P)	117.25	37.79	210	63

1926-1929

Stock Index	Value 1929	Value 1925	Growth	τ
Total (S&P)	51.42	21.48	139	42
Industrials (S&P)	42.19	16.74	152	46
Industrials (DJIA)	352.5	156.66	125	37
Railroads (S&P)	91.27	57.63	76	23
Utilities (S&P)	117.25	45.05	160	48

Sources: U.S. Department of Commerce 1975, series X 487491.

5.3.4 Automation, Underincome and Stock Market Volatility

As I argued in Beaudreau (1998), the OPEC-induced energy crisis put an end to centuries-long energy deepening and, consequently, growing energy rents, the latter being defined as the difference between the marginal value product of energy and its cost. Profit-maximizing producers responded in a number of ways, including automation and offshore production. The 1970's and 1980's were particularly somber decades for stock prices, for obvious reasons.

This, however, began to change in the mid-1980's, as automation and off-shore production began to reap substantial dividends. Labor costs as a percentage of total value added decreased considerably. Stock market prices reflected this. More importantly, as labor costs decreased, stock prices continued their upward spiral.

This raises an important question, namely, how will energy deepening or automation affect profits and expected profits. As it turns out, there is an important difference between the two causes of underincome. Specifically, energy deepening increases potential value added, without increasing actual value added, owing, of course, to the presence of underincome. Depending on the production technology, specifically, on the extent to which lower-level supervisors are fixed inputs, costs per unit of output may not decrease. Consider the case of a machine supervised by a single operator (machine operative). An increase in machine speed, owing say to better lubrication, doubles output per period of time. Will labor costs (supervisor-related) decrease? The answer, of course, is, it depends. It depends whether the producer in question will choose to cut production time in half, or, simply choose to operate the machine at a slower speed.

This, I argue, stands in contrast with nonenergy-based underincome. Take, for example, automation. In this case, the lower-level supervisor referred to in the previous example, is replaced by a control unit (sensors, etcetera). Output is unaffected as a result. In this case, profits will increase as costs fall drastically. However, at the aggregate level, money income decreases, thus putting a damper on future earnings growth. As I shall argue in the next section, this contributed in a non-negligible way to the 2002 stock market crash.

5.3.5 The 2002 Stock Market Crash

The ICT revolution and off-shore relocalization, by reducing variable costs, raised the specter of high profits, and high profits growth. Producers had downsized their labor costs, whether by automation of off-shore relocalization, and were poised to take full advantage of any and all revenue growth. What was true at the individual producer level, however, was not at the aggregate level. In the short run, they were making money, bit not making markets. In fact, they were destroying markets by reducing aggregate money income.

Stock prices reacted much in the same way as they had in the 1920's. Expected higher earnings pushed prices upwards. This is shown in Figure 5.2 which presents the S&P price-earnings ratio from 1921 to 2002. We see that from roughly 1995, the price-earnings ratio increased monotonically, far exceeding its historical average of 15.17. Clearly, investors were banking on a manifold increase in earnings.

Figure 5.2
Standard and Poor's Price-Earnings Ratio 1900-2002

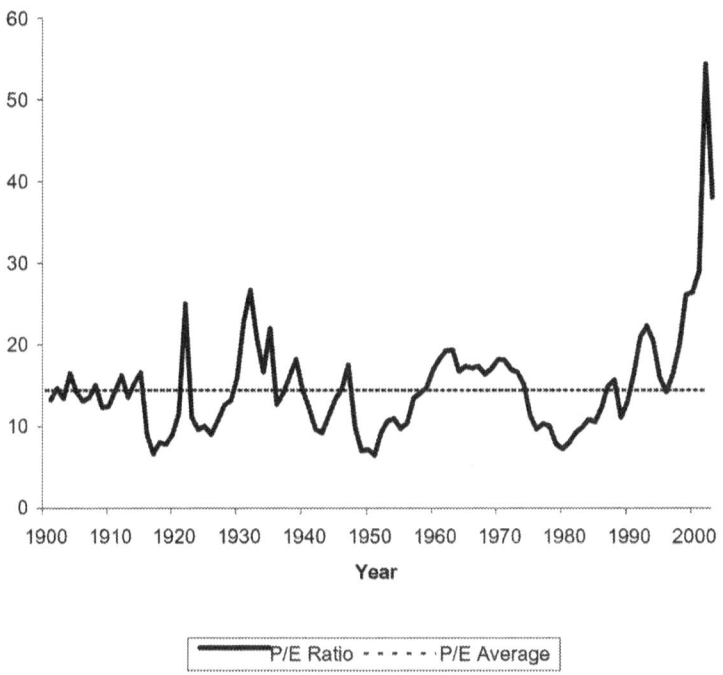

The bubble, however, burst in 2002 when all major stock indexes virtually collapsed. This raises a number of questions, notably why? Why did the stock market collapse after such a stellar performance? Why did prices return to their 1995 level? Why did prices collapse in 2002? Why not in 2000, 2001, or 2002? The answers to these questions, I argue, are analogous to the explanation provided earlier for the 1929 downturn, namely the co-existence of underincome and a policy instrument. In 1929, energy-deepening-based underincome and the proposed changes to tariff contained in the Smoot-Hawley tariff bill pushed prices up. Higher tariffs held out the promise of greater domestic market shares for U.S. companies, and hence, substantially higher profits.

The 2002 stock market collapse, I argue, was analogous. In lieu of energy-based underincome, there was non-energy-based underincome based on ICT and off-shore relocalization. Cost-wise, producers were in an excellent position to "cash-in" on future growth, having reduced their costs significantly. All that was missing was market growth. The latter would result from globalization. As had been the case in the 1920's, earnings growth would be achieved not via "making markets" but by taking advantage of foreign markets. As pointed in Chapter 4, cost-cutting and off-shore relocalization in Western industrialized nations has actually reduced markets (unmaking markets) via lower variable costs.

Globalization held out the promise of greater sales, revenue, and earnings. With little-to-no growth at home, producers turned their attention to foreign marketst. Globalization became the mantra, as producers positioned themselves to "cash-in" on foreign opportunities.

This was not unlike producers in the 1920's who anticipated greater sales from the imposition of higher tariffs. One could also argue that it was not unlike producers in 19th century Great Britain who anticipated greater sales from the abandonment of imperial preference and the beginning of free trade. Common to all three cases is the nature of the game played by producers, namely a Nash money-income (wage) game. Individually, producers, by cutting costs, contribute to "un-making markets." The only way to resolve the problem is via third-party intervention.

As was the case in the past, such schemes are destined to fail, for obvious reasons. Cannibalizing foreign markets cannot, in the long run, work. Foreign producers respond by decreasing their demand for labor, and, in the process, un-make markets. The most recent scheme is no exception.

As it turns out, the Crash of 2002 signaled the beginning of the end. In practical terms, the bull metamorphosed itself into a bear, largely as a result of a fundamental shifts in expectations. Stock prices crashed in response to the collapse of expectations regarding globalization, more specifically, with regard to the income-augmenting capabilities of globalization. Among the mitigating factors were the attacks of September 11, 2001, which put a damper on investor's expectations regarding the new international order. Up until then, expectations ran high, despite a number of setbacks, including several financial crises (Brazil, Mexico, Asia). The attacks of September 11, 2001, however, marked the beginning of renewed tensions in North-South relations. Add to this the events of the WTO meetings in Seattle, the FTAA meeting in Québec City, and the overall deterioration of North-South relations, and you get the reversal of fortunes witnessed in 2002.

5.4 Conclusions

In this chapter, I have examined the implications of underincome for the stock market, paying particular attention to the relationship between underincome and what is commonly referred to as excess volatility in the stock market literature (Shiller 1981,1989). Underincome was advanced as a leading cause of "excess stock price optimism" both in the 1920's and in the 1990's. In both cases, investors had factored in huge productivity gains into the price of shares, on the basis of the widespread belief that commercial policy would provide the wherewithal to increase sales and earnings.

Owing to the fundamental nature of Nash equilibria (underincome), it stands to reason that the resulting optimism, sooner or later, gives way to pessimism, and stock price depreciation. What appears, on the surface, to be excess stock price volatility is nothing more than the presence of technological change and underincome. As such, neither was a bubble, neither was irrational. What was irrational was the belief that commercial policy could resolve the underlying prisoner's dilemma.

In 1929, higher tariffs on imported manufactures held out the hope of higher capacity utilization rates, higher revenues, and higher profits. Domestic merchants would increase their demand for U.S. goods, and decrease their demand for foreign goods. Factories would produce at capacity, and profits would soar. In the 1990's globalization held out similar hope for U.S. manufacturing. New foreign markets would provide outlets for goods produced in intelligent manufacturing plants and the off-shore plants of U.S. multinationals. When globalization failed to live up to expectation, stock prices collapsed.

6

Competition, Cooperation, and "Making the Market"

The only thing that will redeem mankind is cooperation.

—Bertrand Russell

6.1 Introduction

As has been shown, the problem of underincome is intimately tied to the nature of the game played by producers—namely, a Nash game in wages and prices—as well as the nature of the exchange technology, specifically, the residual nature of producer profits. Competition in times of technological change (energy or information-based) is welfare decreasing; cooperation is welfare increasing. Competing producers will, in the presence of a technology shock, fail to "make the market(s)" required to make the transition to the new growth path defined by the technology shock.

This chapter extends the analysis of the role of competition and cooperation in the "making of markets" by examining the historical record in search of examples and/or counterexamples. For example, are there cases in which private Nash producers and merchants did, indeed, overcome the prisoner's dilemma (indeterminacy) described in Chapter 2? If so, when and where?

6.2 Steady State-Based versus Technology Shock-Based Growth

To begin with, it will be important to distinguish between steady-state growth, and technology shock-based growth. Steady-state growth refers to growth which occurs as the result of increases in labor and capital. The capital-labor and, hence, output-labor ratios remain constant. Technology shock-based growth refers to growth which results from a change in technology, pushing the economy on to a new steady-state growth path.

It will be argued here that the problem of "making the market" does not arise in steady-state growth, and, hence, is limited to technology shock-based growth. The reason lies in the very nature of output growth. In technology shock-based growth, output growth is costless (free). Producers' cost structure is not affected, or hardly. Electrification is a case in point.[1] Steady-state growth, on the other hand, affects producers' cost structure. Anticipating an increase in the merchant's orders, profit-maximizing producers will increase their demand for labor, thus increasing ω, operating capital. Money income rises commensurately with output.

6.3 Markets and "Making the Market"

In economics, markets are synonymous with exchange. As exchange exists in myriad forms, so too do markets. Table 2.1 in Chapter 2 provides a non-exhaustive list of the various types of exchange, broken down into two sub-categories, namely non-intermediated and intermediated. The former refers to exchange without the presence of an intermediaries. Examples are barter and monetary exchange. The latter refers to exchange in the presence of intermediaries (specialized traders).

In the case of non-intermediated trade, a necessary condition for a market (exchange) to take place is the presence of the double-coincidence of wants. That is, the presence of two agents each having what the other wants (quality and quantity). As such, the presence of a single agent offering good x and demanding good y is not sufficient.

In the case of intermediated trade, a necessary condition for a market (exchange) to take place is the double coincidence of wants involving agents and specialized traders. In the case of a monetary economy, the agent must have the good the specialized trader deals in, and the latter must have the money the agent wants.

Distinguishing the two cases is the fact that in latter (intermediated trade), exchange involving only one side of the market is required to make the market. The suppliers and demanders of goods (services) are now separated by specialized traders. It is in this sense that one should understand the term, "to make the market," used throughout this book. In the presence of money, specialized traders make the market by trading. By choosing to be active at a particular point in time, specialized traders "make the market," specifically by creating a supply, and a potential demand in the form of money.

It stands to reason that in such an environment, specialized traders are a sine quo non of trade and exchange. Their presence and, more importantly, their dealings, ensure the workings of markets.

6.4 Incentives for "Making the Market"

As was shown in Chapter 2, in a producer-merchant exchange environment where profits are a residual form of factor income, there are no private incentives for producers to "make the market" so-to-speak in response to a technology shock. By increasing unilaterally wages by τ percent, the representative consumption/capital goods producer increases its costs by more than its revenues. Similarly, the merchant has no private incentives to "make the market," that is, increase orders of consumption and capital goods by τ percent. The additional consumption goods would go unsold, thus diminishing—in fact, choking off—the demand for the additional capital goods. Competition, defined here as the Nash wage and price game played by producers, is as such welfare decreasing. Cooperation, on the other hand, is welfare increasing. By increasing wages by τ percent, consumption and capital goods producers, the demand for consumption goods would rise by τ percent. Consequently, the merchant would increase orders of consumption goods by τ percent, thus increasing consumption goods producers' earnings by τ percent, which, in turn, would lead to a τ percent increase in the demand for capital goods.

This raises an interesting question, namely, are there counterexamples? Are there non-steady state growth examples where private-maximizing agents "made the market?"

6.5 Making the Market: The Historical Evidence

Underincome, as defined above, is a classic prisoner's dilemma. There are no private incentives to "make the market," resulting in a situation in which no market is made. In fact, in times of technological change, producers are more likely to "unmake markets," by cutting employment. Taking the argument one step further, underincome is, in essence, an impossibility result. That is, starting from a position of complete autarky in which agents do not trade, there are no private incentives for intermediated trade to develop spontaneously—that is, on its own. In a Nash environment, merchants have no incentives to "make a market" by purchasing output from a producer, in the hope of selling it. Only if merchants can somehow coordinate their behavior will a "market be made."

It is generally believed that markets, as we know them today, originate in the early 19th century (Polanyi 1944), having no precedents in human history. Karl Polanyi remarked:

> Market economy implies a self-regulating system of markets; in slightly more technical terms, it is an economy directed by market prices and nothing but market prices. Such a system capable of organizing the whole of economic life without outside help or interference would certainly deserve to be called self-regulating. These rough indications should suffice to show the entirely unprecedented nature of such a venture in the history of the race. (Polanyi 1944, 124)

Prior to this, trade in general was controlled by what Morris Silver refers to as "royal merchants," that is, merchants in the service of the court. As pointed out in Chapter 2, the problem of "making the market" was orthogonal to royal merchants, the market being dictated by the court, and financed, in large measure, by various taxes.

The relevant question is whether non-royal merchants existed, and if so, did they, collectively, make markets? *In Economic Structures of Antiquity*, Morris Silver, professor emeritus of economics at the City College of New York, presents evidence which suggests the presence of non-royal merchants in the ancient Mediterranean.

> The question has not been posed as "Did the ancient Mediterranean world know private merchants?" because rulers and officials who engaged in commercial activities may or may not have been public enterprisers in the sense that their enterprises with their profits belonged to the "public," that is, to the nation at large. To illustrate, in about the middle of the second half of the second millennium, the ruler of Cyprus, in requesting payment for a shipment of lumber, complained to Pharaoh that "the people of the land murmur against me" (Liverani). Why did people "murmur"? Were the "murmurers," so to speak "stockholders" in a royal export enterprise? Or were they independent merchants who had not received payment for their lumber and asked their king to intercede with Egypt's king in their behalf? (Silver 1999, 1)

Unfortunately, the presence of a handful of non-royal merchants does not make a convincing case for the existence of spontaneous markets (merchants), as defined above. The reason is simple, namely, the absence of a legal (read: legitimate) market. The presence of important gains from trade is not a sufficient condition for merchant-intermediated markets to emerge, as pointed out above. In the absence of coordination and communication, individual merchants have no private incentives to "make the market" so to speak.

That royal merchants vastly outnumbered non-royal merchants, I maintain, is consistent with the impossibility theorem implicit in the concept of underincome. Private, non-royal, intermediated markets were inexistent in antiquity for the problem of underincome. This is not to say, however, that barter or monetary trade did not occur. Private agents in antiquity no doubt traded, and, in many cases, the trade involved a form of money (salt, precious metal, etcetera). Organized non-royal merchant trade did not, however.

The impossibility theorem predicts that private, intermediated market activity will, owing to the problem of "making the market," fail to emerge, and, if it does somehow emerge, it will be characterized by crises of oversupply and underincome. The shift from mercantilism to industry (first industrial revolution) in late 18th century/early 19th century Great Britain bears this out. As pointed out in Chapter 3, steam power increased greatly the productive power of U.K. industry, especially the textiles industry. While individual producers trebled, or in some cases, quadrupled productivity and productive capacity, they failed to provide the wherewithal to "make markets" commensurately. Producers made goods, not markets, with the result that the early 19th century was characterized by recurrent commercial crises. Capacity far exceeded supply and demand. Producers responded not by heeding Robert Owen's and Thomas Malthus' pleas to "make markets," but by petitioning the government to repeal the Corn laws, and thus open markets until then closed to U.K. manufactures. For the next half century, government-sponsored foreign trade would provide the markets private producers, owing to underincome, could not make.

Another example of the impossibility theorem at work is the second industrial revolution, which, like the first, involved a massive increase in productive capacity due to electrification. U.S. consumption and capital goods producers could make more goods than ever before. However, they failed to make the necessary markets. As pointed out in Chapter 3, producers responded by calling on the federal government to further restrict access to the U.S. market to foreign competitors. Unlike their 19th century U.K. counterparts who had called upon Sir Robert Peel to provide them with access to foreign markets, U.S. producers demanded a larger share of the existing domestic markets (Smoot-Hawley Tariff Bill of 1929). A resounding failure, the government, with the blessing of the business community, undertook to reform the workings of markets by fiat (National

Industrial Recovery Act of 1933). Herbert Hoover referred to this as the "associative state." As it turns out, this was the first ever attempt to formally address the problem of underincome, and, as such, the impossibility theorem. As pointed out in Chapter 3, producers would be required to make the market. Wages would be determined by fiat; put differently, the government would, indirectly, make the market—that is, via its wage and price policy.

In 1935, the Roosevelt administration's attempt at wage and price setting was found to be unconstitutional, thus spelling the end of wage and price policy as a means of "making the market" in the United States. This led to the second "New Deal," with its emphasis on collective bargaining. The Wagner Act of 1935 provided U.S. workers with the constitutional right to bargain collectively (i.e. collective bargaining). If markets could not be made by directly setting wages, then they would be made indirectly, by providing workers with the wherewithal (e.g. social-legal institutions) to increase their real wage.

The wisdom of the New Deal, specifically of the right of workers to bargain collectively as a "market-making device" was borne out in the post-WWII period, when energy deepening continued unabated, increasing conventionally-defined productivity monotonically. With wages tied to productivity, markets (real income) increased commensurately with output and capacity, ushering in a golden era of U.S., and indeed, world capitalism.

6.6 Mercantilism, Industrialization, and Making the Market

The shift from mercantilism to industrialization at the end of the 18th century witnessed an important change in the organization of exchange, one that goes beyond the emergence of a new class of economic agents, namely the capitalists (owners of capital). Specifically, it altered the way in which "markets were made," so to speak. Under mercantilism, sovereigns typically made the market, issuing money (coinage), purchasing goods and services, and obtaining revenue via taxation. The key market indicator, as far as merchants were concerned, was the sovereign's planned expenditures. If for whatever reason it increased, then merchants would increase their orders of goods.

This changed with the advent of industrialization. Now, producers, via their purchases of factor inputs, especially labor, would contribute to making the market. Soon, the key market indicator as far as merchants were concerned was wage income—ignoring the foreign sector. Government no longer played the pivotal role it had previously.

Qualitatively speaking, this represented a fundamental change in economic organization, from a game-theoretic point of view. Government, which had from Mesopotamia to the 18th century, played an important—integral—part in coordinating economic activity, would now play a minor role, at least according to classical and neoclassical political economy. The invisible hand of the market, according to Adam Smith, would ensure the efficient allocation of scarce resources.

What about coordination failures? How would the "invisible hand of the market" coordinate behavior, and, in the process, solve the underlying coordination failure. The answer was simple, namely, that coordination failures simply did not exist. Following basic utilitarianism, the greater good of society is achieved by individuals behaving selfishly. That is, playing Nash strategies.

6.7 Policy Implications

The policy implications of these findings are far-reaching. Specifically, competition as defined here (Nash wage and price behavior on the part of producers and merchants) is welfare decreasing in times of technological change. Wage and price-setting Nash producers have no private incentives to make the markets required for a successful transition to the new, higher equilibrium growth path. Put differently, while steady-state growth can be supported as a competitive equilibrium; however, technology shock-based growth cannot. The latter, it therefore follows, requires some form of third-party intervention (e.g. government).

This leads us to conclude that market formation, whether from scratch or from an existing level of output, is a social phenomenon, one characterized by non-negligible indeterminacies, and one requiring some form of governmental (third-party) coordination.

6.8 The Political Economy of Making Markets: A Game-Theoretical Approach

The market impossibility theorem has important implications for industrialization, specifically, the process of industrialization. Take, for example, the case of a country wanting to industrialize. Suppose there are n producers and one merchant. The relevant question is, will a national market emerge? Will the n producers, starting from scratch, generate enough operating capital (income) to allow the country to take off, so to speak? Strictly speaking, the answer, in light of the market impossibility theorem, is no. Nash wage and price setting producers have no private incentive to "make the market," owing, once again, to the nature of the game played by producers. In the absence of a market, I as an individual producer, have no incentive to produce (purchase intermediate inputs, labor, energy, etcetera), knowing that there is no one to buy my product. The resulting Nash equilibrium is characterized by inertia.

This result, I maintain, provides a compelling rationale for export-led growth. Given the failure of domestic markets to create income (operating capital) commensurately to a country's ability to produce (add value), by turning to foreign markets, a country can circumvent the relevant prisoner's dilemma. By targeting existing markets, the associated indeterminacy disappears.

Japan, I argue, provides a good example of this. From very early on in its history, Japanese industrial policy focused on export-led growth. The Ministry of International Trade and Industry (the order of the words suggesting causality), encouraged manufacturers to target existing markets, especially North America and Europe. The results are there for everyone to see, and, to a large extent, emulate. Throughout the past three decades, the Japanese economy has performed remarkably well. Unemployment has been consistently low, the emphasis here being on the word consistently.

> Since the establishment of the Ministry of International Trade and Industry (MITI) in 1949, from a reorganization of the former Ministry of Commerce and Industry, MITI has played a central role in the development of policies on industry and international trade, through the implementation of many measures under its jurisdiction. Responding to changes in social and business requirements, MITI has made efforts to attain a more affluent society, and improve the quality of life in Japan. (www.meti.go.jp/english)

Coordination failures, one could argue, militate against the spontaneous emergence of markets in underdeveloped countries, which, in the end, corroborates claims by international institutions such as the IMF and the World Bank that export-led growth dominates all other types of growth.

6.8.1 A Global Prisoner's Dilemma?

Export-led growth, à la Japan and China, raises an important exchange-related problem, namely, is the global economy not heading for a generalized collapse. As jobs are being destroyed in the North, and created in the South, global wage income falls. In addition to producing goods and services, producers in the North make markets by way of their decisions in labor markets. The latter act as a signal to merchants, who, in turn, place orders with producers. As production is transferred off-shore, the question of underincome arises. Specifically, could export-led growth, at least conceptually, lead to global underincome?

This question raises another important issue, namely, the role of exchange-related matters in the trade literature. Put differently, why have these questions been ignored in the voluminous globalization literature? Why has trade been studied in terms of real models (Ricardo and Heckscher-Ohlin) that abstract from monetary exchange?

I do not have answers to these questions, except to say that some writers have alluded to these issues. Take, for example, John Culbertson of the University of Wisconsin–Madison, who, in the following passage, refers to the role of markets (monetary exchange) in international trade:

> Our present-day economics fails to recognize the importance of demand and markets—and thus exaggerates what production alone can accomplish. Yet a nation's productive capacities are decisively limited by the levels and kinds of domestic demand and its access to foreign markets. But in the United States, we persistently fail to see the importance of our vast, prosperous and accessible domestic market. We don't appreciate the key role the demand side of our domestic market has played in generating economic growth for our country. (Culbertson 1986, 123)

This can be understood in terms of the producer-merchant model of exchange presented in Chapter 2. Specifically, a "vast, prosperous and accessible" internal market increases ω, the overall level of outstanding merchant credit, which increases the likelihood of success. In other words, the market is made.

6.8.2 Making the Market and The Problem of Economic Development

Our findings have important implications for the problem of economic development, specifically with regard to the role of merchants and markets in growth. The theory of economic development, being a derivative of mainstream, neoclassical analysis, ignores the problem of making markets. Supply creates its own demand. There is no mention of merchants, money income, etcetera.

This, I argue, is a non-negligible oversight in so far as the problem of economic development is concerned. Perhaps the single, most-important problem facing developing economies is the existence of markets, as defined here. Upstart producers have few options in so far as selling their goods and services are concerned. A well-developed merchant sector is, as pointed out in Chapter 2, a necessary condition for the creation of wealth.

This raises the question of policy. How can a developing economy overcome the market/merchant constraint? There are, at the very least, two options, the first being some form of government intervention. In this case, the government would have to substitute itself for private merchants, creating outlets for producers. The second option would consist of some form of integration with a developed (industrial) economy, or put differently, with an existing market. In this case, producers would be free-riding, so-to-speak on existing markets.

One could argue that such a view underlies the current free-trade rhetoric, specifically the view that free trade creates wealth. Clearly, from a material point of view, free trade cannot create wealth. It can, however, by providing an outlet for goods and services, by providing a merchant sector that is otherwise either inexistent or underdeveloped. Where it is inexistent, free trade provides producers with access to markets.

There is, however, a downside, namely that producers in underdeveloped countries, not having access to developed national markets, have to compete with foreign producers, some of which may be highly competitive. In this case, free trade can be welfare-decreasing, as foreign producers may crowd out local producers.

6.9 The Demand for and Supply of Coordination

The last issue I would like to address in this section is the demand for and supply of coordination. Prior to industrialization, coordination was provided by government (mercantilism). The latter's ubiquitous presence can, as such, be viewed as a testimony of the demand for—or need of—coordination.

With the end of mercantilism came the end of government as a provider/supplier of coordination, so to speak. Markets and prices were "freed," from government intervention. The problem, I maintain, is that while the end of mercantilism brought about the end of the supply of government-provided coordination, it did not, however, bring about the end of the demand for coordination. If anything, nascent industrialization increased the demand for coordination, as shown in Chapter 2. Ironically, at a time at which the demand for coordination was at its highest, the supply of coordination was at its lowest.

6.9.1 Alternative Forms of Coordination

Coordination failures in the Nash wage and price game described above owe to the inability of producers to coordinate productivity-based wage increases or price decreases. As a result, producers find that they are unable to "vent" all their output, owing to underincome.

It therefore follows that anyone or anything that could potentially increase overall income and sales will be welcomed by producers and merchants, and could, as such, be the basis for stock price appreciation. For example, anticipated export growth could push stock prices higher as producers factor in the increased sales, profits and earnings. A new technology could do likewise.

The point of the matter is that producers and merchants—not to mention investors—finding themselves in a sub-optimal Nash equilibrium, will be receptive to any and all possible solutions. This leads me to argue that in the absence of government-based coordination, markets will be highly responsive to what I refer to as trends and tendencies, and, moreover, will be highly volatile. Anything that could, at least potentially, increase sales will be a candidate. The recent rash of speculative bursts on Wall street, I maintain, can be attributed, in part, to this phenomenon. Take, for example, the Asian miracle in the early 1990's. One could argue that the Asian miracle, by raising expectations, contributed to increasing economic activity. Producers, anticipating an increase in trade, increased output, which, like all self-fulfilling prophecies, led to increased exchange. The bottom fell out, however, when the anticipated returns on investment failed to materialize.

Another example is the dot.com frenzy. In this case, the catalyst was electronic commerce (e-commerce). Investors banked on e-commerce replacing traditional forms of merchandizing (storefront). When the anticipated gains failed to materialize, the market collapsed.

6.10 Conclusions

As I have tried to argue in this chapter, social situations (settings) are, in general, fraught with indeterminacies, with coordination failures, with prisoner's dilemma. As a species, we have developed, over time, numerous coordination devices such as government, culture, and customs. Trade, as described here (producer-merchant framework), is no exception to the rule. Since time immemorial, it has been characterized by various indeterminacies, ranging from the problem of specialization itself, to the problem of underincome.

The point of this chapter is that, regardless of one's ideological bend, coordination failures abound in economics, requiring some form of intervention. Formally, there exists a demand for and a supply of coordination. In the absence of institutional providers of coordination (government), the supply of coordination will be provided by the group itself, and will, more often than not, be based on fads.

This view differs fundamentally from Shiller (1989) who attributes excess stock price volatility to changes in public opinion. While public opinion may, in fact, influence stock prices, it is our opinion that stock price movements have a real underlying cause, one that may, owing to underincome, escape the attention of the traditional analyst.

7

The Future of Exchange

Government and Cooperation are in all things the laws of life. Anarchy and competition, the laws of death.

—John Ruskin

7.1 Introduction

As shown in the previous chapter, the current information and communications technology (ICT) revolution is doing more than rendering animate forms of supervision, and, consequently, traditional forms of labor, obsolete; it is altering, in a fundamental way, the very nature of exchange. As traditional workers are phased out of production processes, wage income as a share of overall producer costs is declining, as is producers' demand for working capital. In the process, supervision-related factor payments (share of output to supervision—inanimate) becomes a residual form of income, paid out once merchants (read: retailers) take delivery of the merchandise (paid with merchant operating capital).

These changes raise a number of interesting questions. For example, will these changes lead to a return to the exchange technology of old, that is, prior industrialization? In the limiting case in which there is no animate supervision (upper- and lower-level), will the demand for operating capital on the part of producers cease to exist. In short, will we witness a return to the exchange technology of the cottage-industry era?

How will this affect expenditure? As the functional distribution of income is increasingly skewed towards capital, will consumption decrease? Theoretically, this need not necessarily be the case, given that investors both spend and save. Nonetheless, there is the possibility that, owing to the fact that workers, at least historically, had a greater marginal propensity to consume than investors, consumption will decrease.

This chapter examines these issues, paying particular attention to the question of future exchange technologies. As producers withdraw from their traditional role of making the market, how will exchange evolve? It is shown that while this will affect the nature of the Nash game played by producers and merchants, it will not change the outcome. The level of outstanding credit will continue to be the equilibrium of a Nash game, albeit with fewer players. Where things may change, however, is with regard to traditional Keynesian concerns such as the consumption-investment mix. As the functional income is increasingly skewed toward the owners of capital, the demand for consumption goods may decrease, provoking a Keynesian-style recession.

7.2 Evidence

Prior to the energy crises in the 1970's and 1980's, process engineers focused the bulk of their attention on what refer to as energy deepening, a process that takes on a number of forms, the most common of which is machine speed-ups. A speed-up is the process where, by increasing the speed at which machines function, producers can get more output from a fixed supply of inputs (capital and labor).[1] As Alfred Chandler put it:

> In modern mass production, as in modern mass distribution and modern transportation and communications, economies resulted more from speed than from size. It was not the size of the manufacturing establishment in terms of number of workers and the amount and value of productive equipment, but the velocity of throughput and the resulting increase in volume that permitted economies that lowered costs and increases output per worker and per machine. (Chandler 1977, 23)

The energy crises put an end to energy deepening (Beaudreau 1995,1998,1999a), and, more importantly, altered the very scope of process engineering, away from energy-deepening and over to computer-based automation. This is sometimes referred to as the ICT (Information and Communications Technology) revolution. As pointed out in Chapter 4, inanimate forms of supervision (control technologies) replaced animate forms. In short, computer-based control technologies replaced and continue to replace human beings.

Engineering consulting firms have, as a result, broadened their expertise, focusing, for the most part, on energy and automation.

7.2.1 Case Study: The Pulp and Paper Industry

Take, for example, the case of the pulp and paper industry. Consider the following description of the services Siemens offers to pulp and paper firms.

> Pulp and paper Drawing on its experience in industries requiring batch or continuous control of manufacturing plant, Siemens Automation Drives is well equipped to provide full automation and process control solutions to the pulp and paper industry. Batch process solutions and recipe modeling techniques as well as continuous process control. Simple, stand alone, PLC and PC based control of discrete machinery or plant wide control of all aspects of production, from goods inwards, through mill automation and control to quality and control and warehousing. Full project management and on-site support. Full automation solution from switch gear and motors through to drives, controls and software. Fully validated, automated solutions including user documentation and β. Easy reconfiguring of control systems reduces the cost of changes to your batch production and process architecture. Easy to use human machine interfaces Built in redundancy for critical operations Totally integrated Automation to ensure that automation components communicate Seamless integration, in single or multiple plants Paper, pulp and board mills, printers and packaging manufacturers rely on Siemens wherever flexible and reliable process control is needed. By maximizing throughput and minimizing the cost of re-engineering to accommodate changes as plants grow or new products require manufacturing, Siemens AD provides the paper industry with improved product quality, better yields and Totally Integrated Automation on a plant wide basis. (www.siemens-industry.co.uk/industrial/pulp.asp)

Siemens is but one of a number of consulting engineering firms offering a broad range of automation services to the pulp and paper industry. The end result is, as Jeremy Rifkin has pointed out, the "end of work" as traditionally defined. Animate, human supervision has been, and continues to be replaced, by control systems, with the result that pulp and paper plants are now, for all intents and purposes, workerless. Specialized ICT technicians can, with the help of process engineers, operate plants.

Do these findings generalize to the manufacturing sector as a whole? Do they generalize to the economy as a whole? Clearly, the answer depends, in large measure, on automation itself, specifically, on the extent to which it generalizes to the economy as a whole. Clearly, some sectors are more conducive to automation than others, owing to the very nature of the supervisory function. In general, if it is relatively simple, then automation is, in most cases, appropriate, and vice-versa.

Some sectors, particularly the service sectors, will resist automation, for obvious reasons.

7.2.2 U.S., German, and Japanese Manufacturing

To see just how close OECD manufacturing is to worker-less production processes, I projected current trends in output and productivity growth (i.e. production worker productivity) into the future. For example, from 1974 to 1993, U.S. manufacturing value added increased at an annual rate of 0.80 percent per annum. Over the course of this period, value added per production worker and value added per non-production worker increased at 1.74 and 0.14 percent per annum, respectively. In 1993, U.S. manufacturing value added stood at $307,724,500,00 (constant 1985 dollars). The number of production workers and non-production workers stood at 11,731,70 and 6,512,700, respectively.[2]

Now, suppose, for the sake of argument, that value added were to stay at its 1993 level for the next 50 years. It being the case that output per production worker is increasing at an average annual rate of 1.74 percent, it stands to reason that the demand for production workers would decrease at a proportional rate. Each individual production worker (i.e. lower-level supervisor) is assigned more responsibility within a given department/firm. Figure 7.1 presents the resulting projections of production worker employment in U.S. manufacturing. We see, for example, that in the zero-growth scenario, the number of production workers goes from 11,731,700 in 1993 to 6,815,244 in 2043, a 42 percent drop.

Figure 7.1
Projected Employment, U.S. , Japanese, and German
Manufacturing 1993–2043

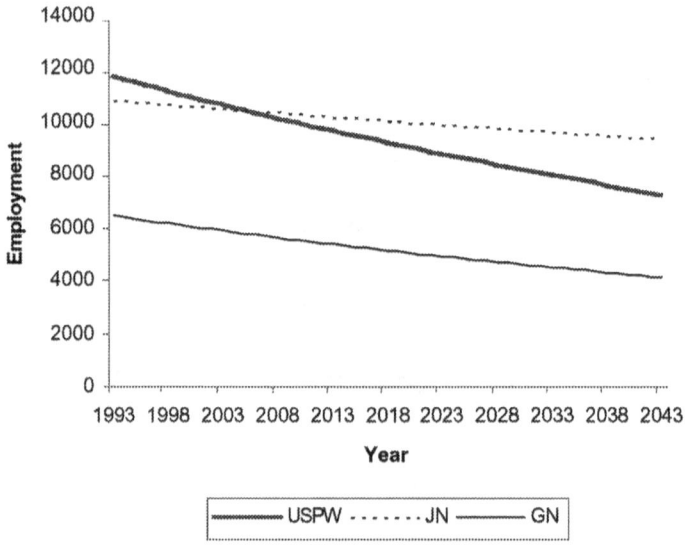

Similar projections were made using German and Japanese manufacturing data from 1974 to 1988. Figure 7.1 presents projected total employment in German manufacturing for the no-growth scenarios. In the no-growth scenario, total employment goes from 6,732,000 in 1988 to 1,847,553 in 2043. The Japanese case is also similar. In the no-growth scenario, total employment in Japanese manufacturing will go from 10,962,000 in 1989 to 1,685,123 in 2043, while in the growth scenario, it will go from 10,962,000 in 1989 to 9,416,205 in 2043. In 2043, projected Japanese manufacturing value added will be 458 percent greater than in 1989, yet total employment will be 14 percent lower.

Advances in control technology have and will continue to render lower-level supervisors obsolete. If current trends are maintained, the demand for animate lower-level supervisors will continue to fall well into the 21st century. As pointed out above, if U.S. manufacturing value added continues to grow at 0.80 percent per annum, and value added per production workers continues to grow at 1.74 percent per annum, then by 2043, the demand for production workers will have fallen by 11 percent. In other words, if production workers become redundant at an average annual rate of 1.74 percent, then it is just a matter of time before they are completely phased out of modern production processes. This, however, does not apply to non-production workers. As I showed above, non-production worker productivity has not risen nearly as fast as that of their production worker counterparts. This reflects, in part, the fact that control technologies have not yet entered the realm of upper-level supervisors. For example, it is not clear, at least not at this point in time, that control technologies will one day replace conventionally-defined managers. Will robots one day supervise robots? While this sounds far-fetched, it is important to remember that production and non-production workers are, first and foremost, suppliers of supervisory skills. SMART manufacturing may, in time, give way to SMART management.

Evidence that automation is decimating the ranks of white-collar as well as blue-collar employees is fairly commonplace in the popular press, not to mention the business literature. Take, for example, the following passage taken from a story in the *Montreal Gazette* entitled "Office job squeeze is the worst—Survey."

> The vision of computers replacing armies of office employees has become one of the most commonplace images as telephone companies, banks and corporate empires announced cuts of office workers and administrators. But those announcements told only half the story, leaving out hiring. The cuts remained anecdotal evidence of an apparent trend. Now a massive study of Quebec businesses appears to confirm the labor analysts' impression that the functions of office workers and middle managers are being squeezed out of the shifting labor market, indicating that it may be happening faster than many experts thought–and is far from over. (*Montreal Gazette*, September 14, 1996, 15)

7.3 The Future of Exchange

Unlike the rest of this chapter, and indeed, the rest of this book, this section is speculative in nature. Specifically, I ask and attempt to answer the following questions, namely, how will these changes affect the exchange technology, and, if so, what will the consequences? Will the exchange process be made easier or harder? Will underincome be more or less probable?

7.3.1 Automation and Exchange

Here, I begin by listing the changes that I believe are important to understanding future developments. The first consists of the decline in labor costs in total costs. The demand for operating capital on the part of producers continues to decline as a result. The ratio of up-front to residual factor payments continues to decrease as a result. Over time, it is believed that this ratio will tend towards zero, as inanimate, automated forms of supervision replace animated, human forms. Claims to output (value added) will become increasingly concentrated in the hands of the owners of capital.

The functional distribution of income, however, is not the issue, at least, not as far as this chapter—and, indeed, the book—is concerned. At issue, however, is the effect such a change will have on the exchange technology in general, and on the complex system of signaling between producers and merchants, described by Equations 2.1-2.13 in Chapter 2. According to Equation 2.9, merchants base their orders on the expected level of aggregate (consumption and capital good producers) producer operating capital (i.e. ω). An increase in the latter typically leads to an increase in the former.

As animate, human forms of supervision are phased out of production processes, this signal will disappear (i.e. in the long run). The question then becomes, what signals will then guide merchants' orders? Whereas previously, the level of money income (aggregate operating capital) was determined jointly by producers and merchants, now, it will be determined solely by the latter. A merchant will now have to anticipate what his/her counterparts will be doing. For example, take the case of a car dealer (merchant). Whereas in the past, he could base his orders on the level of producer operating capital (correlated with employment), now he cannot. Rather, he, like all other merchants, is forced to estimate the demand for all goods and services, which, in turn, will determine the level of income, and, as such, the demand for automobiles. Producers will no longer affect the level of output and income. This raises further questions. For example, will the resulting economy be more or less stable? Will it be more or less prone to expectation-related perturbations?

These are difficult questions to answer, especially in the absence of any precedent. As pointed out in Chapter 2, in the pre-industrial era, merchants typically took their signals from the state (emperor, government, church). The merchant class, as was shown, developed, largely in response to the demand, on the part of the state, for goods and services. As went the state, so went the affairs of the merchant class. In the industrial era, the signals came primarily from the producers, by way of the demand for labor (wage income). An increase in wage income would typically signal an increase in the demand for goods and services, and, consequently, an increase in merchants' orders.

7.3.2 The Possible Breakdown of Exchange

Now, let us proceed to combine this with the increasingly skewed functional distribution of income referred to earlier. Assuming that the demand for consumption goods (and services) on the part of the owners of capital is finite and limited, there exists a clear and present danger that Western industrialized economies could lapse into a recession/depression at least as, if not more, severe than that of 1929. As the demand for consumption goods decreases, the demand for capital goods will decrease for obvious reasons. Assets will be worthless, given the absence of exchange. In short, an economic cataclysm of epic proportions.

Could something be done to prevent this? Could forward-looking producers and merchants take corrective measures? The answer is both yes and no. In the short run, they could do what 19th century producers and merchants did in Great Britain, namely, exchange surplus output against foreign assets, known otherwise as free trade. The problem of underincome in the first part of the 19th century, as pointed out in Chapter 2, led merchants to find outlets abroad for their surplus goods (textiles, cutlery, etcetera). Throughout the ensuing period, Great Britain ran a widening current account surplus, and, consequently, a widening capital account deficit. The problem, however, is that the supply of foreign assets are finite. Once all of the earth's assets are concentrated in the hands of a few, then the initial problem returns.

The only viable solution, I believe, would involve a radical overhaul of the functional distribution of income, one based on scientific, not political (read: bargaining), principles. As I have argued (Beaudreau 1998,1999a), the current distribution of income bears little relationship to actual physical productivity, as defined by basic mechanics and thermodynamics. Conventionally-defined labor and capital are both organizational variables, affecting productivity through η, the level of second-law efficiency (i.e. of the various production processes). The only physically-productive factor input is energy in its many forms.

An example of this would be an energy standard. As organization-related activities are energy based, it follows that the distribution of income could, at least theoretically, follow an energy standard. A factor's share of total output would, as such, track, its contribution, energy-wise. Capital's energy contribution would, as such, be based on the overall energy cost of producing the capital goods themselves. For example, if the capital good has an expected lifetime of 10 years, then, it could be the interest rate plus depreciation rate times the initial capital cost.

A producer's desire to produce say x units of a good would be signaled to merchants (i.e. the market) via the accompanying demand for credit, the receipts of which would be used to purchase the energy input (variable input). Merchants would, in turn, demand goods and services, based largely on the overall level of outstanding credit.

If energy is seen as a public good, then the rents from energy would be public, and, consequently, be deployed via public choice mechanisms. If, on the other hand, it is a private good, then the owners of energy would be entitled to these rents.

7.4 Conclusions

The ICT revolution has and continues to do more than changing material processes in industry. It is also changing exchange technologies in western industrialized democracies. As I have attempted to show in this chapter, the reduction of variable, up-front costs relative to total costs alters fundamentally the nature of the merchant's problem. Overall up-front variable costs acted as a signal, conveying important information to merchants.

As pointed out in this Chapter, there is reason to believe that the relevant exchange technology in Western industrialized nations will regress back to that of pre-industrial times, where coordination failures abounded, and the responsibility of "making markets" fell squarely on the shoulders of governments.

Summary and Conclusions

In 1923, Boston merchant, Edward A. Filene, provided a blueprint for "successful living in the machine age."

> In the future a really big business success on the basis of mass production and mass distribution will be impossible except as it makes for both high wages and low prices... Low wages and high prices manifestly cut down that widespread and sustained buying power of the masses without which mass production sooner or later defeats itself. In other words, the business man of the future must produce prosperous customers as well as saleable goods. He cannot think of business as an adventure in getting money from the masses of people who, in one way or another for which he has no responsibility, have got money from someone else. His whole business policy must look forward to creating great buying power among the masses. Otherwise mass production cannot succeed. The business man of the future must fill the pockets of the workers and consumers before he can fill his pockets. (Filene 1924, 201)

In this book, using a combination of historical analysis, game theory, and statistical analysis, an attempt was made to provide an analytical basis for the problem of underincome as seen by Filene, by Henry Ford, by Jean-Charles Léonard Sismonde de Sismondi, by Thomas Malthus, and by countless others. To begin with, an attempt was made to overcome the shortcomings of existing models of a monetary economy. More specifically, a producer-merchant model of monetary exchange was developed and used to examine the game-theoretical aspects of output and income growth in the presence of technological change. It is believed that the resulting model provides a convenient framework to examine the problems and issues raised by Filene, Ford, and the others.

Further, the resulting model was also used to examine a number of current problems, ranging from the ICT revolution to globalization to the future of exchange. As I have attempted to demonstrate, the exchange technology has an important bearing on the workings of an industrial economy. The shift from a pre-industrial economy to an industrial one had non-negligible effects on the transactions technology, especially with regard to the question of "making the market." The ICT revolution and globalization are having non-negligible effects

on the transactions technology, and, as such, on the workings of modern industrialized economies.

The resulting model, we believe, begins to address the problems raised years
ago by Williford I. King and others regarding the very way in which the economics profession chose to study money. Among other things, it puts merchants into
the analysis, with interesting results, especially with regard to expectations.
Ignored for the most part, merchants play an integral role in industrial economies, often affecting the course of events. As shown in Chapter 2, merchant
expectations can, *ceteris paribus*, alter output and income.

Also, it contributes to the literature on emergence of economic organization.
Whereas economic theory sees economic organization as emerging spontaneously, this book, drawing on the historical record, points to its non-spontaneous
origins, owing, in large measure, to myriad coordination failures. Evidence of the
non-spontaneous origins of economic organization was also provided.

By way of conclusion, I would like to comment on the fundamental underlying thesis of this book, namely the ubiquitous nature of coordination failures in
trade and exchange, and in social behavior in general. Coordination failures have
been, for the most part, ignored in theoretical models of exchange, owing, in
large measure, to ideological considerations. As coordination failures require the
presence of third-parties and third-party intervention, they are "government
increasing." By denying their existence, one denies the need for coordination and
government intervention. Such was the case in 19th century Great Britain and in
20th century America. While theoretically sound, the National Industrial Recovery Act of 1933, an enlightened piece of legislation, was rejected on ideological
grounds. Interestingly, today, the NIRA is seen as a blight in the history of U.S.
economic policy.

The proof of the pudding, as the saying goes, is in the eating. In addition to
providing an analytical framework for the analysis of the first and second industrial revolutions, the model presented in Chapter 2 provides the wherewithal to
examine the future of exchange, in light of two recent developments, namely the
ICT revolution (third industrial revolution) globalization, the latter referring to
the massive off-shore relocalization by G-6 multinationals of footloose manufacturing activity. As pointed out in Chapter 7, these two developments do not
auger particularly well for the future. In fact, as far as exchange technology is concerned, they could conceivably lead to a return to pre-industrial (cottage industry) times, where merchants and sovereigns made markets. In the limiting case in
which there are no up-front costs (worker-less society), producers will no longer
be involved in making markets. Merchants will inherit the onerous responsibility

of "making the market." As producers move in this direction (no up-front costs), markets will be "unmade," as variable costs are reduced, if not totally eliminated. As Thornstein Veblen pointed out, producers will respond by cutting output, and not price, the result of which will be a decrease in overall economic activity.

Endnotes

Chapter 2

1. Among the shortcomings of this literature is the ubiquitous presumption that specialization is independent of markets (exchange technology). Put differently, the decision to specialize (as opposed to remaining autarkic) is viewed as independent of the relevant exchange technology. Clearly, a more reasonable approach would be to model the problem simultaneously. That is, agents would decide to specialize or not, based on the exchange technology in place, and the exchange technology in place would depend on whether agents specialized.

2. See Silver (1994) for evidence of non-governmental media of exchange.

3. Where markets replace government hierarchy, merchants may be former functionaries.

4. One could argue that in the absence of the desire on the part of Homo-sapiens-sapiens to dominate others (empire-build), the world today would be quite different, to say the least.

5. By spontaneous trade, it should be understood trade between individual agents.

6. One could go as far as arguing that public choice-related trade and civilization are synonymous, civilization being defined as urban-rural specialization dominated by centralized government (administration and defence) and religion. See Dudley (1991), Chapter 1 for more.

7. It could be argued that trade, both in the 19th and 20th centuries, was an amalgam of forced and spontaneous, with the latter increasing more rapidly than the former.

8. Such was the underlying theme of Adam Smith's "Wealth of Nations."

9. One could argue that the merchant's problem is no different from the producer's problem (services). Merchants add value to goods/services not unlike any producer in the value added chain. To do so, however, is to ignore the special place merchants play, individually and collectively, in western industrialized (read: market) economies. First, the merchant is the last link between consumers and producers. Second, the merchant, unlike an upstream or downstream producer, deals with thousands if not millions of customers. Third, the merchant's demand for goods and services is determined not by downstream producers, but by all producers, via their factor market behavior).

10. In early civilizations, governments issued money (currency). This function, however, was, with the founding of the Bank of England in 1645, transferred to the private sector. Nonetheless, the government—in this case, the...—still exercised control over the supply of money. A good example of this is the *Bank Charter Act of 1843*, which saw limits imposed on the amount of credit the Bank of England could issue.

11. One could assume the existence of numerous merchants, without affecting any of the results. I shall return to this later.

12. For the sake of simplicity, I ignore, to begin with, energy and all organizational inputs other than capital and labor (Beaudreau 1998,1999a). This is motivated, in large part, by exchange-related concerns, namely the preponderance of labor and capital costs in overall costs (i.e. of value added).

13. This mimics the short-run production analysis found in standard neoclassical production theory (fixed price).

14. This is consistent with the observed practice of remitting profits once revenues are re-ceived, and outstanding debts have been paid. Unlike all other costs, profits are a residual form of factor payment.

15. Clearly, this is a simplifying assumption, having no effect whatsoever on the outcome.

16. Given the heterogeneity of agents (producers and merchants, these states of nature should be seen as averages, describing central tendancy. Clearly, not all merchants and not all producers think and reason alike.

17. This, I argue, explains why large banks typically have an economics department whose chief role is forecasting. Specifically, as banks have a double stake in output, via the producer and the merchant, they stand to lose the most.

18. I implicitly assume that the economy is growing at a rate n, where n is the rate of growth of the labor force.

19. Another way of looking at this is in terms of public goods. By raising wages (τ percent), producer *ic* creates a public good in the form of money income. Assuming that workers consume all n goods, it follows that all other consumption goods producers will benefit by way of higher sales.

20. Specifically, they would capture $\tau\,[V_c + V_k]$.

21. Paul Sweezy examined a similar question in his 1939 article entitled "Demand under Conditions of Oligopoly." See Sweezy (1939).

22. Perhaps this explains the asymmetry that one typically finds in trade negotiations, where countries promote their exports, but fail to promote foreign imports, thus depriving their citizens of the much-anticipated gains from trade.

23. Alternatively, financial corporations could come into being, buying and selling foreign debt.

Chapter 3

1. Workers, it therefore follows, do not perform physical work; instead, they perform organizational work, the latter being somewhat of an oxymoron.

2. This is consistent with neoclassical production analysis where energy- and organization-related technology shocks enter A, the technology parameter. That is, they are parametric in nature. Workers, it therefore follows, do not perform physical work; instead, they perform organizational work, the latter being somewhat of an oxymoron.

3. Conventionally-defined labor productivity is defined as the ratio of output (value added) to labor input.

4. Remember that power looms/spindles operated on a continuous-time basis.

5. That product prices do not fall automatically or instantaneously may owe to the fact that producers choose not to produce at the new, higher capacity, giving rise to a decidedly Keynesian outcome where quantities, not prices, adjust.

6. Perhaps the best way to understand these two types of responses is in terms of Albert Hirschman's notion of "voice or exit," with "voice" corresponding to the National Regeneration Society and the Repeal of the Corn Laws, and "exit" corresponding to communes and communism.

7. One could go as far as arguing that U.K. merchant interest in the repeal of the "Corn Laws" as manifested by the merchant-led "Anti-Corn Law League," is evidence, albeit circumstantial, of the problem of underincome. As a number of historians have pointed out, it was the primarily the merchant class, not the various labor organizations, that petitioned and campaigned to have the "Corn Laws" repealed, the underlying idea being that by opening the U.K. up to foreign "corn," it would be better able to export its textiles abroad. Such concerns, I maintain, are indicative of the presence of generalized excess capacity in the U.K. economy in the 1840's and, hence, the problem of underincome.

8. Ford's Highland Park plant, one could argue, marks the crossover from high-throughput continuous-flow production processes powered by either water or steam power, to extremely- high-throughput continuous-flow production processes powered by electricity. Put differently, the looms and spinning jennies of the early 19th century, powered by steam power, constituted high-throughput, continuous-flow production processes. The electric-powered stamping machines, the electric-powered material handling systems, the electric powered assembly lines, on the other hand, constituted extremely-high (in a comparative sense), continuous-flow production processes.

9. It need be pointed out that not all of this represents a net increase in energy consumption as electric drive had not completely displaced steam drive in industry.

10. As pointed out earlier, this view of productivity is archaic. Labor is not productive in the physical sense; instead, it is productive in the organizational sense. As such, labor productivity is analogous to management productivity.

Chapter 4

1. One could argue that this process is ongoing. Producers continue to replace antiquated human-supervision based production technologies with "smart technologies." Manufacturing employment has decreased continuously since the 1970's. See Rifkin (1995) for more on the "End of Work."

2. This has been referred to and continues to be referred to as rationalization.

Chapter 5

1. Wealth is defined as transformed raw materials, transformation requiring both energy and organization.

2. Nye's view ignores the problem of making the market. Implicitly, capacity is a sufficient condition for output and income, and, consequently, expenditure.

Chapter 6

1. Energy is seen as manna from heaven, which, given the nature of fossil-fuel and hydraulic-based energy, is not too far from the truth.

Bibliography

Aghion, Philippe and Peter Howitt. 1998. *Endogenous Growth Theory*. Cambridge, MA: MIT Press.

Akin, William E. 1977. *Technocracy and the American Dream, The Technocratic Movement, 1900–1940*. Berkeley, CA: University of California Press.

Alting, Leo. 1994. *Manufacturing Engineering Processes*. New York, NY: Marcel Decker Inc.

Anderson, F.J., N.C. Bonsor and B.C. Beaudreau. 1982. *The Economic Future of the Forest Products Industry in Northern Ontario*. Thunder Bay: Royal Commission on the Northern Environment.

Archibald, Chris, and Richard Lipsey. 1958. Monetary and value theory: A critique of Lange and Patinkin. *Review of Economic Studies*.

Baines, E. 1835. *The History of the Cotton Manufactures*. London.

Beaudreau, Bernard C. 1995. The impact of electric power on productivity: The case of U.S. manufacturing 1958–1984. *Energy Economics* 17: 231–236.

Beaudreau, Bernard C. 1996a. *Mass Production, The Stock Market Crash, and The Great Depression: The Macroeconomics of Electrification*. Westport, CT: Greenwood Press.

Beaudreau, Bernard C. 1996b. R&D: To Compete or to Cooperate. *Economics of Innovation and New Technology* 4:173–186.

Beaudreau, Bernard C. 1998. *Energy and Organization: Growth and Distribution Reexamined*. Westport, CT: Greenwood Press.

Beaudreau, Bernard C. 1999a. *Energy and the Rise and Fall of Political Economy*. Westport, CT: Greenwood Press.

Beaudreau, Bernard C. 1999b. Electric power, Keynes, and the $4.86 Pound : A reexamination of Britain's return to the Gold Standard. *Journal of European Economic History* 28.

Beaudreau, Bernard C. 2003. On the Origins of Large-Scale Specialization and Exchange: A Game-Theoretical Approach. Université Laval, Department of Economics, manuscript.

Beiser, Arthur. 1983. *Modern Technical Physics*. Menlo Park, CA: The Benjamin/ Cummings Publishing Company.

Bell, Spurgeon. 1940. *Productivity, Wages and National Income*. Washington, DC: Brookings Institution.

Bental, Benjamin and Benjamin Eden. 1996. Money and inventories in an economy with uncertain and sequential trade. *Journal of Monetary Economics* 445-459.

Berg, Maxine. 1980. *The Machinery Question and the Making of Political Economy*. Cambridge: Cambridge University Press.

Berndt, Ernst and David O. Wood. 1975. Technology, prices and the derived demand for energy. *The Review of Economics and Statistics* 259–268.

Betts, John E. 1989. *Essentials of Applied Physics*. Englewood Cliffs, NJ: Prentice-Hall.

Blanchard, Olivier and Stanley Fisher. 1989. *Lecture on Macroeconomics*. Cambridge, MA: MIT Press.

Bose, Bismal K. 1967. Introduction to microcomputer control, in Bose, Bismal K. ed. *Microcomputer Control of Power Electronics and Drives*. New York, NY: IEEE Press.

Bresnahan, Timothy and Manuel Tratjenberg. 1992. General purpose technologies: Engines of growth. *National Bureau of Economic Research Working Paper* No. 4148.

Butt, John. 1971. *Robert Owen: Prince of Cotton*. Newton Abbott: David and Charles.

Casson, Lionel. 1984. *Ancient Trade and Society.* Detroit, MI: Wayne State University Press.

Chase, Stuart. 1934. *The Economy of Abundance.* New York, NY: MacMillan Company.

Chandler, Alfred D. Jr. 1977. *The Visible Hand, The Managerial Revolution in American Business.* Cambridge, MA: Harvard University Press.

Clower, Robert. 1967. A Reconsideration of the Microeconomic Foundations of Macroeconomic Theory. *Western Economic Journal* 6:1-8.

Clower Robert W. 1995. *Economic Doctrine and Method: Selected Papers of R. W. Clower.* Aldershot: Edward Elgar Publishing Co.

Christensen, L. R., and D.W. Jorgenson. 1970. U.S. Real Product and real Factor Input. *The Review of Income and Wealth.*

Clark, James D. 1985. *Pulp Technology and Treatment for Paper.* San Francisco, CA: Miller Freeman Publications.

Cleveland, Cutler J., Costanza, R., Hall, Charles, and Kaufmann, R. 1984. Energy and the U.S. economy: A biophysical perspective. *Science* 225:890–897.

Clower, Robert and Peter Howitt. 1998. Keynes and the Classics: An End of Century View. in Ahiakpor, James C.W. *Keynes and the Classics Reconsidered.* Boston, MA: Kluwer.

Clower, Robert. 1967. A reconsideration of the microfoundations of monetary theory. *Western Economic Journal* 1–19.

Coleman, Matthew J., ed. 1991. *Energy Engineering and Management in the Pulp and Paper Industry.* Atlanta, GA: TAPPI.

Culbertson, John. 1986. The folly of free trade. *Harvard Business Review* 122-128.

David, Paul A. 1990. The dynamo and the computer: An historical perspective on the modern productivity paradox. *American Economic Review, Papers and Proceedings* 355–361.

Devine, Warren D. 1990. Electricity in information management: The evolution of electronic control. in Schurr, Sam. H. et al. (eds.). *Electricity in the American Economy*. Westport CT: Greenwood Press.

Douglas, Clifford H. 1933. *Social Credit*. New York, NY: W.W. Norton and Company.

Douglas, Clifford H. 1951. *The Monopoly of Credit*. Liverpool: K.R.P. Publications.

Dudley, Leonard. 1991. *The Word and the Sword: How Techniques of Information and Violence Have Shaped Our World*. London: Basil Blackwell.

Farmer, Roger E.A. 1996. *Macroeconomics of Self-Fulfilling Prophecies*. Cambridge, MA: MIT Press.

Fielden, John. 1833 (1972). National regeneration. in Carpenter, Kenneth E. (ed.) *The Factory Act of 1833*. New York, NY: Arno Press.

Filene, Edward A. 1924. *The Way Out: A Forecast of Coming Changes in American Business and Industry*. New York, NY: Doubleday, Page and Co.

Filene, Edward A. 1931. *Successful Living in This Machine Age*. New York, NY: Simon and Schuster.

Finley, Moses I.1973. *The Ancient Economy*. Berkeley, CA: University of California Press.

Fischer, Stanley. 1974. Money and the production function. *Economic Inquiry* 12:517–533.

Fisher, Irving. 1911. *The Purchasing Power of Money*. New York, NY: MacMillan.

Fisher, Irving. 1930 *The Stock Market Crash and After*. New York, NY: Macmillan.

Ford, Henry. 1926. Mass production. *Encyclopedia Britannica* 13:821–823.

Friedman, Milton and Anna J. Schwartz. 1963. *A Monetary History of the United States 1867–1960*. New York, NY: National Bureau of Economic Research.

Garnsey, Peter, Keith Hopkins, and C.R. Whittaker (eds.). 1963. *Trade in the Ancient Economy*. Berkeley, CA: University of California Press.

Gollop, F.M., and Jorgenson, D.W. 1980. U.S. productivity growth by industry, 1948–1973," in Kendrick, J.W., and Vaccara, B.N. (eds). *New Developments in Productivity Measurement and Analysis*. Chicago, IL: National Bureau of Economic Research.

Grant, Michael and Rachel Kitzinger (eds). 1988. *Civilization of the Ancient Mediterranean, Greece and Rome*. New York, NY: Charles Scribner's Sons.

Griliches, Zvi 1995. The Discovery of the Residual: An Historical Note, National Bureau of Economic Research, Working Paper 5348.

Gullickson, William and Michael J. Harper. 1988. Multifactor productivity in U.S. manufacturing, 1949–1983. *Monthly Labor Review* 18–28.

Hahn, Frank. 1973. On transaction Costs, inessential sequence economies and money. *Review of Economic Studies* 40:449-61.

Helpman, Elhanan (ed.). 1988. *General Purpose Technologies and Economic Growth*. Cambridge MA: MIT Press.

Helpman, Elhanan and Manuel Trajtenberg. 1994. A time to sow and a time to reap: Growth based on general purpose technologies," *National Bureau of Economic Research Working Paper* No. 4854.

Henderson, James M. and Richard E. Quandt. 1980. *Microeconomic Theory*. New York, NY: McGraw Hill.

Hicks, John. 1935. A suggestion for simplifying the theory of money. *Economica*.

Hills, Richard L. 1970. *Power in the Industrial Revolution*. Manchester: Manchester University Press.

Hills, Richard L. 1989. *Power from Steam, A History of the Stationary Steam Engine*. Cambridge: Cambridge University Press.

Honeyman, Katrina. 1982. *Origins of Enterprise: Business Leadership in the Industrial Revolution*. Manchester: Manchester University Press.

Hounshell, David A. 1984. *From the American System to Mass Production 1800–1932: The Development of Manufacturing Technology in the United States.* Baltimore, MD: The Johns Hopkins University Press.

Howitt, Peter, and Robert Clower. 2000. The emergence of economic organization. *Journal of Economic Behavior and Organization* 41: 55-84.

International Labour Office. 1996. *Globalization of the Footwear, Textiles and Clothing Industries. Report for Discussion at the Tripartite Meeting on the Globalization of the Footwear, Textiles and Clothing Industries: Effects on Employment and Working Conditions,* Geneva.

Jones, Larry D. and A. Foster Chin. 1991. *Electronic Instruments and Measurements.* Englewood Cliffs, NJ: Prentice Hall.

Jorgenson, D.W. 1983. Energy prices and productivity growth. in Schurr, S. et al. (eds.) *Energy, Productivity, and Economic Growth.* Cambridge, MA: Oelgeschlager, Gunn, and Hain.

Jorgenson, D.W. 1981. The role of energy in productivity growth. in Kendrick, J.W. (ed.) *International Comparisons of Productivity and Causes of the Slowdown.* Cambridge MA: MIT Press.

Jorgenson, D.W. and B. Fraumeni. 1981. Relative prices and technical change, in Berndt, E.R. and B Field (eds.). *Modelling and Measuring Natural Resource Substitution.* Cambridge, MA: MIT Press.

Keynes, John Maynard. 1936. *The General Theory of Employment, Interest and Money.* London: Macmillan.

King, Williford I. 1920. Circulating capital: Its nature and relation to public welfare. *American Economic Review* 10:738-754.

Krueger, Alan. 1999. Measuring Labor's Share, Princeton University, Industrial Relations Section, Working Paper 413.

Lacey, Robert. 1986. *Ford: The Men and the Machine.* Boston, MA: Little, Brown and Company.

Laidler, David. 1977. *The Demand for Money: Theories and Evidence.* New York, NY: Dun-Donnelley.

Laidler, David. 1990. *Taking Money Seriously and Other Essays*. Cambridge: MIT Press.

Laidler, David. 1993. *The Demand for Money: Theories, Evidence and Problems* (4th ed.). New York, NY: HarperCollins College Publishers.

Law, John. 1705. *Money and Trade Considered With a Proposal for Supplying the Nation with Money*. Edinburgh: Andrew Anderson.

Maddison, Angus. 1998. Growth and slowdown in advanced capitalist economies: Techniques of quantitative assessment. *Journal of Economic Literature* 25:649–698.

Malthus, Thomas.R. 1827. *Principles of Political Economy Considered with a View to Their Practical Application*. New York, NY: Augustus M. Kelley.

Mannisto, Heikki. 1991. Who can afford to save energy?"in Coleman, Matthew J. ed. *Energy Engineering and Management in the Pulp and Paper Industry*. Atlanta, GA: TAPPI.

Mansfield, E., J. Rapoport, J. Schnee, S. Wagner, M. Hamburger. 1971. *Research and Innovation in the Modern Corporation*. New York, NY: W.W. Norton and Co.

Marshall, Alfred. 1890. *Principles of Economics*, 8th Edition. London: MacMillan.

Marotta, Michael. 1994. Some questions on the origins of coinage. *Classical Numismatic Review*.

Marx, Karl. 1867. *Das Capital*. Chicago, IL: Encyclopedia Britannica. 1992.

Mathias, Peter. 1969. *The First Industrial Nation: An Economic History of Britain 1700–1914*. London: Methusen Co.

Merill, Milton R. 1990. *Reed Smoot: Apostle in Politics*. Logan, UT: Utah State Press.

Mirowski, Philip. 1988. Energy and energetics in economic theory: A review essay. *Journal of Economic Issues* 22:811-830.

Mirowski, Philip. 1989. *More Heat Than Light, Economics as Social Physics, Physics as Nature's Economics*. Cambridge: Cambridge University Press.

Mitchell, B.R. 1988. *British Historical Statistics*. Cambridge: Cambridge University Press.

Mokyr, Joel. 1994. Technological change, 1700–1830. in Floud, Roderick and McCloskey, Donald, (eds.) *The Economic History of Great Britain Since 1700*, Volume 1: 1700–1860. Cambridge: Cambridge University Press.

Moulton, Harold G. 1938. *Financial Organization and the Economic System*. New York, NY: McGraw-Hill.

Mowery, D.C. and N. Rosenberg. 1989. *Technology and the Pursuit of Economic Growth*. Cambridge: Cambridge University Press.

Musson, A.E. 1976. Industrial motive power in the United Kingdom, 1800-70. *Economic History Review* 29:415–439.

Nye, David. 1983. *Henry Ford: Ignorant Idealist*. New York, NY: Gateway-Associated Faculty Press.

Nye, David E. 1990. *Electrifying America: Social Meaning of a New Technology*. Cambridge, MA: MIT Press.

Odum, H.T. and E.C. Odum. 1976. *Energy Basis for Man and Nature*. New York: McGraw-Hill.

Owen, Robert. 1967. *The Life of Robert Owen*. London: Cass.

Owen, Robert. 1817. *A New View of Society and Other Writings*. London: J.M. Dent and Sons, Ltd.

Parguez, A. and M. Seccareccia. 2000. The credit theory of money: The monetary circuit approach. in Smithin, J. (ed.) *What is Money?* New York, NY: Routledge.

Patinkin, Don. 1956. *Money, Interest and Prices*. New York, NY: Harper and Row.

Pigou, Arthur C. 1917. The value of money. *Quarterly Journal of Economics* 37:38–65.

Pigou, Arthur C. 1949. *The Veil of Money.* London: Macmillan and Co.

Polanyi, Karl. 1944. *The Great Transformation.* New York, NY: Rinehart and Company.

Pringle, Heather. 1998. The cradle of cash-types of money and usage of money historically. *Discover.*

Pullen, J.M. and G.O. Smith. 1997. Major Douglas and Social Credit: A reappraisal. *History of Political Economy* 29:219–273.

Radelet, Steven and Jeffrey Sachs. 1998. The Onset of the East Asian Financial Crisis, National Bureau of Economic Research, Working Paper 6088.

Ricardo, David. 1817. *The Principles of Political Economy and Taxation.* New York, NY: Everyman's Library.

Rifkin, Jeremy. 1995. *The End of Work.* New York: G.P.Putnam's Sons.

Robertson, Ross M. 1973. *History of the American Economy.* New York, NY: Harcourt, Brace and Jovanovich.

Romer, Paul M. 1987. Crazy explanations for the productivity slowdown. *NBER Macroeconomics Annual 1987*163–202.

Romer, Paul M. 1990. Endogenous technological change. *Journal of Political Economy* 98:s71–s102.

Romer, Paul M. 1986. Increasing returns and long-run growth. *Journal of Political Economy* 94:1002–1037.

Romer, Paul M. 1994. The origins of endogenous growth. *Journal of Economic Perspectives* 3–22.

Rosenberg, Nathan. 1972. *Technology and American Economic Growth.* Armonk, NY: M.E. Sharpe.

Rosenberg, Nathan. 1983. The effects of energy supply characteristics on technology and economic growth. in Schurr, Sam et al. (eds.). *Energy, Productivity and Economic Growth*. Cambridge, MA: Oelgeschager, Gunn and Hain.

Rosenberg, Nathan, and L.E. Birdzell, Jr. 1986. *How the West Grew Rich: The Transformation of the Industrial World*. New York, NY: Basic Books.

Scott, Howard et al. 1933. *Introduction to Technocracy*. New York, NY: The John Day Company.

Shiller, Robert. 1981. Do stock prices move too much to be justified by subsequent changes in dividends? *American Economic Review* 71:421–436.

Shilller, Robert. 1989. *Market Volatility*. Cambridge MA: MIT Press.

Silver, Morris. 1995. *Economic Structures of Antiquity*. Westport, CT: Greenwood Press.

Sismonde de Sismondi, Jean-Charles Léonard. 1819. *Nouveaux principes d'économie politique*. Paris: Calmann-Lévy.

Smith, Adam 1776. *An Inquiry into the Nature and Causes of the Wealth of Nations*. Chicago, IL: Encyclopedia Britannica.

Sowell, Thomas. 1972. *Say's Law, An Historical Analysis*. Princeton, NJ: Princeton University Press.

Starr, Ross M., and Maxwell B. Stinchcombe. 1999. Exchange in a network of trading posts. In Graciela Chichilnisky (ed.). *Markets, Information and Uncertainty: Essays in Economic Theory in Honor of Kenneth J. Arrow*. Cambridge UK: Cambridge University Press.

Stearns, Peter. 1993. *The Industrial Revolution in World History*. Boulder, CO: Westview Press.

Stern, David I. 1993. Energy and economic growth in the USA. *Energy Economics* 137–151.

Stiglitz, Joseph E. 1990. Symposium on bubbles. *Journal of Economic Perspectives* 13-18.

Sweezy, Paul M. 1939. Demand under conditions of oligopoly. *Journal of Political Economy* 47:568-73.

Tatom, J. 1982. Potential Output and the Recent Productivity Decline," *Economic Review of the Federal Reserve Bank of St-Louis* 64:3–15.

Temin, Peter. 1997. Two views of the British industrial revolution. *Journal of Economic History*.

Thweatt, William O. 1979. Early formulators of Say's law. *Quarterly Review of Economics and Business* 19:79-96.

Thomas, Woodlief. 1928. The economic significance of the increased efficiency of American industry. *American Economic Review* 18:122–138.

Tugwell, Rexford G. 1927. *Industry's Coming of Age*. New York, NY: Columbia University Press.

Tylecote, Mabel. 1957. *The Mechanics Institutes of Lancashire and Yorkshire before 1851*. Manchester: Manchester University Press.

United Nations. 1960–1988. *Industrial Statistics Yearbook*. New York, NY: United Nations.

U.S. Department of Commerce. 1975. *Historical Statistics of the U.S.: Colonial Times to 1970, Bicentennial Edition*. Washington, DC: U.S. Bureau of the Census.

U.S. Department of Commerce. 1960–1988. *Annual Survey of Manufactures*. Washington, D.C.: U.S. Bureau of the Census.

U.S. Department of Commerce. 1986. *Survey of Current Business*. Washington, DC: U.S. Bureau of Economic Analysis.

Varian, Hal R. 1992. *Microeconomic Analysis*. New York, NY: Norton.

Veblen, Thornstein. 1921. *The Engineers and the Price System*. New York, NY: Augustus M. Kelley.

Wallace, Neil. 1988. A dictum for monetary theory. *Federal Reserve Bank of Minneapolis Quarterly Review* 22:20-26.

White, Eugene N. 1996. *Stock Market Crashes and Speculative Manias.* Brookfield, VT: Edward Elgar Publishing.

Wicksell, Knut. 1898. *Interest and Prices, A Study of the Causes Regulating the Value of Money.* London: Macmillan and Co.

Williamson, Stephen D. 1996. Sequential markets and the suboptimality of the Friedman rule. *Journal of Monetary Economics* 37.

0-595-32879-2